12

DATE DUE

# PAUL CÉZANNE

by Barbara Sheen

**LUCENT BOOKS**
*A part of Gale, Cengage Learning*

Detroit • New York • San Francisco • New Haven, Conn • Waterville, Maine • London

**LIBRARY OF CONGRESS CATALOGING-IN-PUBLICATION DATA**

Sheen, Barbara.
    Paul Cezanne / by Barbara Sheen.
        pages cm -- (Eye on art)
    Summary: "These books provide a historical overview of the development of different types of art and artistic movements; explore the roots and influences of the genre; discuss the pioneers of the art and consider the changes the genre has undergone"-- Provided by publisher.
    Includes bibliographical references and index.
    ISBN 978-1-4205-0858-1 (hardback)
    1.  Cézanne, Paul, 1839-1906--Juvenile literature. 2.  Painters--France--Biography--Juvenile literature.  I. Title.
    ND553.C33S49 2012
    759.4--dc23
    [B]
                                                                    2012022861

Lucent Books
27500 Drake Rd
Farmington Hills MI 48331


ISBN-13: 978-1-4205-0858-1
ISBN-10: 1-4205-0858-X

Printed in the United States of America
1 2 3 4 5 6 7 16 15 14 13 12

# CONTENTS

# Foreword

Some thirty-one thousand years ago, early humans painted strikingly sophisticated images of horses, bison, rhinoceroses, bears, and other animals on the walls of a cave in southern France. The meaning of these elaborate pictures is unknown, although some experts speculate that they held ceremonial significance. Regardless of their intended purpose, the Chauvet-Pont-d'Arc cave paintings represent some of the first known expressions of the artistic impulse.

From the Paleolithic era to the present day, human beings have continued to create works of visual art. Artists have developed painting, drawing, sculpture, engraving, and many other techniques to produce visual representations of landscapes, the human form, religious and historical events, and countless other subjects. The artistic impulse also finds expression in glass, jewelry, and new forms inspired by new technology. Indeed, judging by humanity's prolific artistic output throughout history, one must conclude that the compulsion to produce art is an inherent aspect of being human, and the results are among humanity's greatest cultural achievements: masterpieces such as the architectural marvels of ancient Greece, Michelangelo's perfectly rendered statue of *David*, Vincent van Gogh's visionary painting *Starry Night*, and endless other treasures.

The creative impulse serves many purposes for society. At its most basic level, art is a form of entertainment or the means for a satisfying or pleasant aesthetic experience. But art's true power lies not in its potential to entertain and delight but in its ability to enlighten, to reveal the truth, and by doing so to uplift the human spirit and transform the human race.

One of the primary functions of art has been to serve religion. For most of Western history, for example, artists were paid by the church to produce works with religious themes and subjects. Art was thus a tool to help human beings transcend mundane, secular reality and achieve spiritual enlightenment. One of the best-known, and largest-scale, examples of Christian religious art is the Sistine Chapel in the Vatican in Rome. In 1508 Pope Julius II commissioned Italian Renaissance artist Michelangelo to paint the chapel's vaulted ceiling, an area of 640 square yards (535 sq. m). Michelangelo spent four years on scaffolding, his neck craned, creating a panoramic fresco of some three hundred human figures. His paintings depict Old Testament prophets and heroes, sibyls of Greek mythology, and nine scenes from the Book of Genesis, including the Creation of Adam, the Fall of Adam and Eve from the Garden of Eden, and the Flood. The ceiling of the Sistine Chapel is considered one of the greatest works of Western art and has inspired the awe of countless Christian pilgrims and other religious seekers. As eighteenth-century German poet and author Johann Wolfgang von Goethe wrote, "Until you have seen this Sistine Chapel, you can have no adequate conception of what man is capable of."

In addition to inspiring religious fervor, art can serve as a force for social change. Artists are among the visionaries of any culture. As such, they often perceive injustice and wrongdoing and confront others by reflecting what they see in their work. One classic example of art as social commentary was created in May 1937, during the brutal Spanish civil war. On May 1 Spanish artist Pablo Picasso learned of the recent attack on the small Basque village of Guernica by German airplanes allied with fascist forces led by Francisco Franco. The German pilots had used the village for target practice, a three-hour bombing that killed sixteen hundred civilians. Picasso, living in Paris, channeled his outrage over the massacre into his painting *Guernica*, a black, white, and gray mural that depicts dismembered animals and fractured human figures whose faces are contorted in agonized expressions. Initially, critics and the public condemned the painting as an incoherent hodgepodge, but the work soon came to be seen as a powerful antiwar statement and remains an iconic symbol of the violence and terror that dominated world events during the remainder of the twentieth century.

The impulse to create art—whether painting animals with crude pigments on a cave wall, sculpting a human form from marble, or commemorating human tragedy in a mural—thus serves many purposes. It offers an entertaining diversion, nourishes the imagination and the spirit, decorates and beautifies the world, and chronicles the age. But underlying all these functions is the desire to reveal that which is obscure—to illuminate, clarify, and perhaps ennoble. As Picasso himself stated, "The purpose of art is washing the dust of daily life off our souls."

The Eye on Art series is intended to assist readers in understanding the various roles of art in society. Each volume offers an in-depth exploration of a major artistic movement, medium, figure, or profession. All books in this series are beautifully illustrated with full-color photographs and diagrams. Riveting narrative, clear technical explanation, informative sidebars, fully documented quotes, a bibliography, and a thorough index all provide excellent starting points for research and discussion. With these features, the Eye on Art series is a useful introduction to the world of art—a world that can offer both insight and inspiration.

# Introduction

# A Visionary

**P**aul Cézanne was a nineteenth-century artist whose work was ahead of its time. His innovative method of using color to create a feeling of mass and the movement of light, his groundbreaking way of distorting perspective and simplifying forms, and his analytic method of studying his subjects changed the rules of painting forever. Yet the elite French art world of his time did not appreciate his talent. For most of his life, his work was mocked and ridiculed. An 1877 article by French art critic Roger Ballu typifies the kind of scathing criticism Cézanne faced. Cézanne's paintings, according to Ballu, "induce laughter, and yet are lamentable; they display the most profound ignorance of drawing, of composition, of color. When children amuse themselves with paper and colors they do better than this."[1] Not surprisingly, such criticism led Cézanne to doubt his achievements. That, combined with his intense perfectionism, caused him to abandon or destroy many of his paintings in fits of frustration.

## Many Struggles

Lack of recognition as an artist was just one of the many struggles that Cézanne faced. He spent much of his life trying

Cézanne painted *Self-portrait Before a Pink Background* in 1875. Some observers say his expression in this painting shows Cézanne's volatile and emotional personality.

to control his volatile, highly emotional nature and the fits of depression, nervous rage, and bad temper that often overcame him. Making matters worse, he was stubborn, shy, and suspicious of people. Although he had friends and a wife and son, his temperament made it difficult for him to enjoy social situations or spend extended periods of time with anyone before something set him off. In fact, in his later years he so isolated himself that many people assumed he was dead. According to author and art historian Gerstle Mack, "His temper cut him off from the . . . relaxation of social life, the pleasure of good, idle, rambling talk over a glass of wine or a pipe."[2]

Making matters worse, his rustic manners, peasant accent, and wild, unkempt appearance marked him as an outsider in Paris society. In fact, he seemed to revel in his differentness. Not surprisingly, even though he was educated and intelligent, he was often misunderstood both personally and artistically. Upon meeting him at a dinner in 1894, American artist Mary Cassatt wrote a friend:

> When I first saw him I thought he looked like a cut-throat with large red eyeballs standing out from his head in a most ferocious manner, a rather fierce looking pointed beard, quite grey, and an excited way of talking that positively made the dishes rattle. . . . His manners at first rather startled me—he scrapes his soup plate, then lifts it and pours the remaining drops in the spoon; he even takes his chops in his fingers and pulls the meat from the bone. He eats with his knife and accompanies every gesture, every movement of his hand with that implement.[3]

Finances and his family, too, caused him problems. His father was strict and domineering. He disapproved of Cézanne's career choice. Cézanne depended on him for financial support. This gave the older man control over his son's life, a situation that Cézanne greatly resented.

## Changing and Growing

Despite his many struggles, Cézanne never turned his back on art. Painting consumed him. Everything else was secondary. As Mack explains:

> He took absolutely no interest in public affairs or politics; he knew nothing about business. . . . His health gave him no concern at least until he reached his fiftieth year; his love affairs were both fewer in number and less devastating in their intensity than those of other men. . . . It might almost be said that he and his

painting were enclosed in a sort of vacuum, from which everything else in life was excluded.[4]

Cézanne spent most of his life creating a new type of art and was rarely satisfied with his work. Artist Paul Trachtman reports:

In his twenties, he said, "My hair is longer than my talent." At 50, he wrote that "the many studies to which I have dedicated myself have given me only negative results." And in 1905 a year before he died, he lamented, "My age and my health will never allow me to realize the artistic dream I have pursued throughout my entire life."[5]

*The House at Jas de Bouffan* was painted between 1882 and 1885. Cézanne spent most of his life at this house.

Because he was always searching, his painting style changed significantly throughout his life. His early work was dark and dramatic. Then, influenced by Impressionism and painting out in the open air, it became brighter and more colorful. Moving beyond Impressionism, he focused on adding structure and permanence to his artwork by building form with color. Towards the end of his life, he began to depict what he saw in terms of geometric shapes and color, opening the way for abstract art. Cézanne, according to art historian Lawrence Gowing, "was reaching out for a kind of modernity which did not exist."[6] His subjects were equally varied. He painted still lifes, portraits, murals, and landscapes. Often, he would depict the same subject repeatedly, painting it from varied angles, or during different times of day or seasons.

## The Father of Modern Art

Although Cézanne did not gain recognition until late in his life, today his paintings sell for tens of millions of dollars and hang in museums all over the world. More importantly, his work changed the course of art. It created a bridge between Impressionism and the different art movements of the twentieth century. His use of color and oversized brushstrokes inspired Fauvism, a style of modern art characterized by flat, bright colors and wild brushstrokes. His experiments with geometric shapes and perspective and his neglect of anatomical detail led to the rise of Cubism, a style of abstract art in which shapes are broken up and then reassembled in a less realistic form. Since his death, successive generations of artists have studied his work. He has been an inspiration for artists like Henri Matisse, Émile Bernard, Pablo Picasso, Alberto Giacometti, Georges Braque, and Marc Chagall, among others. Cézanne, according to Picasso, "is the father to all of us."[7]

# An Emotional
# Young Man

Paul Cézanne was born on January 19, 1839, in the southern French town of Aix-en-Provence to Louis-Auguste Cézanne and Anne-Elisabeth Aubert, an unwed couple who did not marry until Paul was five years old. He was the oldest of three children, having two younger sisters, Marie and Rose. His father was a successful businessman who spent his life in the pursuit of wealth. At the time of Paul's birth, he owned a hat-making business. In 1848, he became the owner of Aix's only bank.

Even as a toddler, Paul had a hot temper and was prone to brief, unpredictable fits of rage that affected him all his life. When he was not overcome with temper, he was a sweet, happy little boy. He did not show an early passion for art, but he did exhibit talent at it. When he was five years old, he drew a picture with a piece of charcoal on a wall outside his house. Passers-by were amazed by its likeness to a local bridge. "The future painter," his sister Marie Cézanne wrote to Cézanne's son in 1911, "was already discernible."[8]

A few years later, Cézanne's father bought an assortment of secondhand merchandise from a peddler. In it was an old paint set that Louis-Auguste gave to Paul. The boy used the paints to color in pictures in his mother's magazines. No one knows if

According to some sources, Cézanne may have depicted his mother and sister in *Tannhauser Overture* (1869). He was the oldest of three children.

that experience sparked an interest in painting in the boy. Had Louise-Auguste thought it would do so, he never would have given Paul the kit. Cézanne's father thought that painting was an innocent pastime for a child, but no way for a man to earn a living. "Remember," he repeatedly told his son, "we die with genius, but we eat with money."[9]

## A Basket of Apples

In 1852, when Paul was thirteen, he entered the College Bourbon, a secondary boarding school in Aix, where he would remain for six years. Here he met Émile Zola. Zola was born in Paris, France, and would someday become a famous writer. At the time the two met, Zola was a puny, eccentric boy whom the other students bullied and shunned. Cézanne, who was much larger and stronger than Zola, defended him. In gratitude, Zola brought Cézanne a basket of apples.

So began a friendship that would last more than thirty years—and apples would be a frequent subject in Cézanne's still life paintings. Cézanne recalled:

> Zola didn't give a damn about anything. He dreamed. He was stubbornly unsociable. . . . For no reason at all, [the other students] ostracized him. And, in fact, it was on that account that our friendship started. The whole school, big boys and little, gave me a thrashing because I paid no attention to their blackballing. I defied them. I went and talked to him just the same. A fine fellow! The next day he brought me a big basket of apples. There you are, Cézanne's apples . . . they date back a long time.[10]

*Apples* (1878–1879) depicts a fruit that would recur as a subject throughout Cézanne's career.

# AIX-EN-PROVENCE

*Cézanne's birthplace, Aix-en-Provence, is a beautiful and ancient city located in southern France. The surrounding landscape with its olive and pine trees, red earth, cliffs, rivers, plains, mountains and hills, quaint villages, bright sunlight, and seacoast inspired Cézanne throughout his life. An article on the PBS website explains:*

Provence was Cézanne's country: he was at home there as nowhere else. . . . He sought to be a worthy interpreter of the beauty he saw in the Provençal landscape. It was his goal to convey his visual sensations of color, light, and space in the medium of paint, and he succeeded magnificently, producing works of compelling tactile quality and coloristic beauty. In the distinctive country side around his native Aix-en-Provence, Cézanne found the images rich in natural beauty and in emotion that have since become synonymous with his art. Cézanne created some of his most compelling images in the solitude of Provence, including not only landscapes painted outdoors but also portraits and still lifes. Throughout his career, Provence remained a constant source of strength in his struggle to master the means of artistic expression.

PBS.org. "Cézanne in Provence: The Life of Paul Cézanne." www.pbs.org/cezanne/the_life_of_paul _cezanne.html.

## The Inseparables

Émile and Paul offered their friendship to another boy, Jean Baptiste Baille, who later became an engineer. The three became known at school as "The Inseparables." They shared many common interests and spent most of their free time wandering the countryside and swimming in the Arc and Torse Rivers.

Cézanne so enjoyed those happy days that in later years the places where the boys roamed and the theme of swimmers, or "bathers," as he called them, featured prominently in his paintings. After swimming, the boys relaxed on the riverbank, where they talked about their dreams, recited poetry, and discussed art. "We were three friends, three scamps still wearing out trousers on school benches," Zola recalled. He said,

> On holidays, on days we could escape from study we would run away on wild chases cross-country. We had need of fresh air, of sunshine, of paths lost at the bottom of ravines. . . . In the winter, we adored the cold . . . and we went to eat omelets in neighboring villages. In the summer all our meetings took place at the riverbank, for then we were possessed by the water. In the autumn, our passion changed, we became hunters; oh! very innocuous hunters for the hunt was for us only an excuse to take long strolls. The hunt always ended in the shade of the trees, the three of us lying on our backs with our noses in the air, talking freely about our loves. And our loves, at the time, were . . . the poets.[11]

The boys considered themselves rebels. They favored contemporary, nontraditional, romantic writers like Victor Hugo and antiestablishment artists like Gustave Courbet and Eugène Delacroix. Courbet was the leader of the Realistic art movement. Delacroix led the Romantic art movement. Both these artistic movements developed in the mid-nineteenth century in defiance of traditional values. The Realistic art movement focused on portraying in a realistic manner common people performing everyday tasks. Color palettes were limited and paint was often applied to the canvas in thick layers with a palette knife. Romantic artists emphasized the importance of imagination and feeling. They used dramatic brushstrokes to depict the movement of color and light. Both art movements were disdained by the art establishment. It favored Neoclassicism, which was taught in

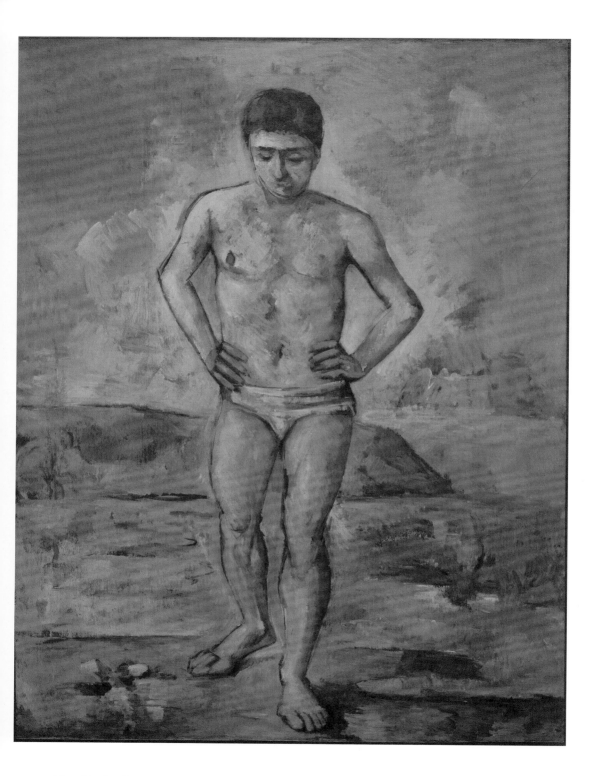

18   Paul Cézanne

French art schools. Neoclassicism drew its inspiration from the art of ancient Greece and Rome. Neoclassical paintings lacked emotion. They told stories or had moral value. Brushstrokes were almost invisible, and the clarity of the outline of a drawing was considered more important than the quality of color.

Early in his painting career, Cézanne studied Delacroix's Romantic style. He said it helped him learn to use color. But during his school years, Cézanne did not consider himself an artist. He frequently decorated notes and letters to Zola with sketches of the boys swimming, but that was all in fun. He wrote poetry, too. He did not take his writing or his artwork seriously. They were, like excursions and discussions with his friends, a source of amusement and a way to express himself.

## A Volatile Personality

The boys often talked about the brilliant futures they dreamed of having. Of the three, Cézanne was the least confident. "Life," he was known to say, "is terrifying."[12] To some degree, life was indeed terrifying for the young man. He suffered from frequent fits of depression and periods of self-doubt. On these occasions, if anyone contradicted his opinions he exploded, insulting his friends, storming off, and isolating himself. The rest of the time, he was kind and generous. If he had any money, he insisted on treating his friends. When they questioned his overindulgence, he joked that if he died suddenly he did not want to leave the few coins he possessed to his parents.

Zola seemed to understand Cézanne and defended the artist's behavior. "When he hurts you," he wrote in a letter to Baille, "you must not blame his heart, but rather the evil demon that beclouds his thought. He has a heart of gold and is a friend who is able to understand us, being just as mad as we, and just as much a dreamer."[13]

Other people were less forgiving. In an effort to keep from repelling others with his outbursts, as he aged Cézanne became more and more of a loner. In some respects doing so kept him

*Opposite page:* In *The Bather* (1885), Cézanne recalls memories of his happy childhood, a prominent subject later in his life.

from being distracted and allowed him to dedicate himself completely to his painting.

# Law Student by Day, Artist by Night

The carefree times "The Inseparables" enjoyed came to an abrupt end in 1858 when Zola was forced to leave school for financial reasons and move to Paris. In November of that year, Cézanne and Baille graduated from the College Bourbon. The two grew apart, but Cézanne and Zola remained friends. They exchanged frequent letters. Cézanne's often included little drawings and watercolor paintings, since he was becoming more and more interested in art. Zola urged his friend to come to Paris and study art. Cézanne liked the idea, but had no money of his own. Besides, as yet he was not fully committed to dedicating his life to art.

Cézanne's father had his own plans for his son. He insisted the young man pursue a lucrative and respectable career, such as banking, business, or law. Cézanne found it easier to do what his father wanted than to stand up to him, so he enrolled in law school.

His studies bored him. As time passed, his dissatisfaction with the law grew and so did his interest in painting. He began to feel more strongly that it was his vocation. Cézanne's letters to Zola at the time were filled with his frustration. In one, he vented his unhappiness in the form of verse; in it, he called his law studies torture and begged the Muses, mythological goddesses who inspire artists, to rescue him.

To ease his frustration, Cézanne took classes at night in the local art school. The teacher was a mediocre artist who had no interest in anything innovative. The curriculum consisted of classes in which the students carefully copied reproductions of old art prints, or sketched and made paintings of plaster-cast figures and of a live male model. Drawing from nature was ignored, as was creative use of color. Cézanne did not distinguish himself

Cézanne hated law school. *The Lawyer (Uncle Dominique)* (1866) may be a comment on that period of his life.

at the school. His work was imaginative and emotional, not at all the kind of work his highly traditional teacher preferred. To supplement his art education, Cézanne often skipped his law classes and visited the little art museum in Aix where he diligently copied the paintings. However, the museum's collection was small and third rate. There were no masterpieces from which Cézanne could learn.

*The Artist's Father, Reading "L'Evénement"* (1866) is a good example of Cézanne's early painting.

Cézanne spent three years in this way. During this time, he renewed his acquaintance with Philippe Solari, a local boy who was also studying in the art school. Solari eventually became a sculptor and created two busts of Cézanne in 1905. Cézanne also met Achille Emperaire. Emperaire was an artist who had dwarfism. Cézanne painted his portrait in the future. Although Cézanne stayed in touch with both men for the rest of his life, their friendship and his life as a law student by day and art student by night was not enough for him. He yearned to join Zola in Paris and take up painting as his career. However, he did not want to confront his father or disappoint him. In a letter to Cézanne, Zola urged his friend to commit himself:

> Is painting only a whim that took possession of you when you were bored one fine day? Is it only a pastime, a subject of conversation, a pretext for not working at law? If this is the case, then I understand your conduct; you are right not to force the issue. . . . But if painting is your vocation—and that is how I have always envisaged it—if you feel capable of achieving something after having worked well at it, then you are an enigma [puzzle] to me. . . . If I were in your place I would want to have the answer, to risk all to gain all, and not float vaguely between two such different futures. . . . One thing or the other, really be a lawyer, or else really be an artist, but do not remain a creature without a name, wearing a toga [a lawyer's robes] dirtied with paint.[14]

# Jas de Bouffan

Despite Zola's urging, Cézanne remained in Aix. In 1859, Louis-Auguste Cézanne bought a large country estate named Jas de Bouffan a few miles west of Aix. For the next forty years, it played a great part in Cézanne's life. The big house with its open shutters and red roof, the farm buildings nearby, the grounds surrounding it with the two rows of chestnut trees, the square pool with its statues of lions and dolphins, and the garden wall surrounding the property were a boundless source of inspiration to Cézanne. He painted them from almost every angle in his ever-evolving painting styles.

Cézanne set up an art studio on the top floor of the house, which he increasingly retreated to and maintained for four decades. Between 1858 and 1866, he also painted a series of panels, some on canvas and some right on the walls of the large salon or main room of the house. One of his earliest works was *The Four Seasons*. It consisted of four tall, narrow paintings of women representing the four seasons. The *Spring* panel depicts a woman in a red dress standing in a garden. The woman in the *Summer* panel is seated surrounded by a pile of fruit. *Autumn*'s woman carries a basket of fruit on her head. Finally, in *Winter*, the woman is sitting beside a fire on a cloudy night. The panels are far from Cézanne's finest work. What makes them interesting is that they are done in the Neoclassic style that Cézanne disdained and Cézanne signed them "Ingres," after Jean-Auguste-Dominique Ingres, the leader of the Neoclassic art movement. Art historians believe Cézanne painted the panels in mockery of Ingres and the traditional art movement. Since Cézanne imagined himself a rebel, such an act is likely. No matter his motivation, the precisely drawn panels with their dark outlines of the figures and their classical decorations are good depictions of the official painting style. They are in marked contrast to all of Cézanne's other work in which the outlines are indistinct.

A fifth painting, *The Artist's Father, Reading L'Evénement* (1866), hung in the middle between the two pairs of *Seasons* (*Spring, Summer*, and *Autumn, Winter*). It is not known who placed the portrait of Louis-Auguste in the middle, but it was most likely Cézanne. It is a better example of Cézanne's early painting style than the *Seasons* panels. It is a larger than life-size portrait of Cézanne's father, who is depicted in the painting full face, seated at an angle on an armchair reading a newspaper. He is dressed in black, with a black cap on his head. The painting is dark and the colors are earthy. The paint is applied almost violently in very thick layers with a palette knife. Hanging behind Louis-Auguste's head is a painting within the painting. It is a small still life, one of Cézanne's earliest.

# THE NEOCLASSIC MOVEMENT AND JEAN-AUGUSTE-DOMINIQUE INGRES

*A*s a young man, Cézanne was disdainful of the Neoclassic art movement, which began in the late 18th century. Neoclassic paintings depicted dramatic scenes from history and mythology, biblical parables, and moral tales using historically correct costumes and settings. Neoclassicism was inspired by the artwork of Nicolas Poussin and Raphael and the writing of Homer.

Jean-Auguste-Dominique Ingres (1780–1867) was the movement's greatest champion. According to an article on the *Jean Auguste Dominique Ingres—The Complete Works* website:

A man profoundly respectful of the past, he assumed the role of a guardian of academic orthodoxy against the ascendant Romantic style represented by . . . Eugene Delacroix. His exemplars, he once explained, were "the great masters which flourished in that century of glorious memory when Raphael set the eternal and incontestable bounds of the sublime in art. . . . I am thus a conservator of good doctrine, and not an innovator.

Ingres's work is characterized by strict composition and clear lines. He believed that quality of line was more important than color, atmosphere, or light. In addition to painting classical themes, he also painted portraits and nudes.

Text excerpt from *Jean Auguste Dominique Ingres—The Complete Works.* www.jeanaugustedominiqueingres.org.

*It is believed that Cézanne painted* Spring *(1859–1862) in mockery of Ingres.*

26  Paul Cézanne

Judging by contemporary photographs of Louis-Auguste, the portrait is a very good likeness. He appears serious and dignified. The only incongruity in the painting is the newspaper Louis-Auguste is reading. It is an antigovernment, antiestablishment newspaper, which Cézanne himself might have read but his traditionalist father scorned. In some respects, the painting serves as a window into Cézanne's feelings towards his father. The dignity of the portrait and its likeness to Louis-Auguste shows how much Cézanne admired his father, while the presence of a radical newspaper shows the artist's resentment towards his father imposing his values on his son.

## A Frustrated Artist

In 1861, Louis-Auguste finally loosened his grip on his son. He let Paul go to Paris and provided him with a small allowance. Cézanne rented a furnished room on Paris's Left Bank not far from Zola's residence. At first, things went well. Cézanne went to the Louvre, one of the world's largest art museums, almost every day, where he studied and copied the works of great artists. He also regularly painted at the Académie Suisse, a studio where artists worked from live models for ten francs a month. The Académie Suisse did not offer formal art instruction. Artists worked as they pleased. At the time, this type of freedom was daunting for Cézanne, who had a vision of what he wanted to paint but he could not always express it on canvas. Art instruction might have helped him. As it was, when his work did not turn out the way he envisioned, he became discouraged and frustrated.

Life in Paris, too, disappointed him. He did not like the crowds, the noise, or the hustle and bustle. The street sounds disturbed him when he attempted to paint. Nor did he feel comfortable around the fashionable, sophisticated Parisians, whom he felt were putting on airs. He missed Aix. He had been in Paris a month when he wrote to a friend in Aix: "I am none too cheerful. I fritter away my life on all sides . . . I thought by leaving Aix I should leave behind the boredom that pursued me.

*Opposite page: The Negro Scipion (1866–1868) is an early painting by Cézanne and differs in many respects from his other portraits.*

Actually, I have done nothing but change my abode, and the boredom has followed me."[15]

It was not long before he was threatening to give up art, go home, and work for his father. Zola tried to convince him to stay, but he, too, became frustrated. In a letter to Baille, Zola wrote:

Paul is still the same excellent capricious [unpredictable] fellow. . . . As proof that he has lost nothing of his eccentricity, I have only to tell you that no sooner had he arrived here than he talked of returning to Aix; to have struggled for three years to make this trip and then to throw it away. . . . Before such unlooked for and unreasonable changes of face, I . . . am at [a] loss. . . . To convince Cézanne of anything is like trying to persuade the towers of Notre Dame to dance.[16]

In an effort to keep Cézanne from leaving, Zola asked the artist to paint his portrait. Cézanne began the project with great enthusiasm. But this, also, did not go well. Cézanne was unhappy with his work. When Zola went to Cézanne's studio for his last sitting, he found Cézanne packing his bag, the painting gone.

In a letter to Baille, Zola described what happened:

I go to his place; when I enter I see the trunk open and the drawers half empty; Paul, with a gloomy face, is piling objects into the trunk in disorder. Then he tells me quietly: "I am leaving tomorrow."

"And my portrait?" I ask him.

"Your portrait," he replies, "I have just smashed. I wanted to retouch it this morning and as it was getting worse and worse, I destroyed it; and I am leaving."[17]

The only thing that was preserved of that work is a charcoal sketch that Cézanne made of Zola. What does remain from this time is a self-portrait that the artist painted from a photograph. The painting shows Cézanne's mental state. In the photo, Cézanne looks calm and gentle. In the painting, Cézanne duplicated his own face, but by elongating the chin, accenting the eyebrows, and changing the expression in the eyes, he gave the picture a troubled, menacing appearance. "In this portrait he appears as he visualized himself. It is the portrait of a man who paid for each hour of hope with days of despair,"[18] author John Rewald explains.

Considering his state of mind, it is not surprising that after only five months in Paris, Cézanne returned to Aix. Throughout his life, he was plagued with the same depression, self-doubt, and dissatisfaction with his work that he felt during his first visit to Paris. As a young man, he allowed his feelings to control him and hamper his work. As time went on, he realized that painting was his true vocation, and he would persevere in spite of these feelings.

# Cézanne and the Impressionists

Upon returning to Aix, Cézanne went to work in his father's bank. He hated it and quickly realized that his heart belonged to art. In November 1862, he returned to Paris. Once there, he yearned for Aix. Cézanne spent most of his life ferrying back and forth between Paris and Aix, painting part of the year in each place. This arrangement worked well for him.

## Clumsy and Unconventional

Cézanne's father was not happy with Cézanne's returning to Paris. He agreed to let him go if he applied to Paris's prestigious École des Beaux-Arts (School of Fine Arts), which was controlled by the Academy of Fine Arts. The Academy was the backbone of the French art establishment. Academy members championed Neoclassicism and vehemently opposed any artwork that did not conform to traditional ideals. Even at this early date, Cézanne's work was nontraditional.

Cézanne failed the entrance exam. The admission committee called his paintings clumsy and unconventional. Upon his rejection, Cézanne resumed work at the Académie Suisse. This time he was fully committed to becoming an artist no matter how discouraged he became. He spent mornings and evenings sketching at the Académie Suisse and the rest of the day painting in his studio. On Sundays, sketchbook in hand, he explored the countryside around Paris with Zola.

## Cézanne's Romantic Period

Cézanne called this early period of his career his romantic period. Much of his work at this time was dark and moody. His painting technique and choice of subjects were influenced by both the Romantic and Realistic art movements. But his finished work did not fit into either category.

*The Murder* (1868) is an example of Cézanne's early Romantic period.

Cézanne slathered black paint on his canvases in thick layers—spreading it, flattening it, and cutting into it with his palette knife much like a builder slaps on wet cement. He called this method *couillarde*, which means daring or manly. The subjects, taken from the depth of his imagination, were often sinister and violent. Paintings depicting death, abduction, orgies, and rape all found their way onto his canvases. *The Murder* (1868) is probably the most dramatic and disturbing. In it, Cézanne portrayed two people brutally slaying a woman. The murderers have no faces, but the victim's face is twisted in pain. The figures and background are dark and foreboding and seem to wash over each other. Only the victim's arms and head are distinct. The paint is laid on thickly and violently, and the colors are somber and muddy. As a description by the Walker Art Gallery, Liverpool, England, where the picture has been on display since 1964, explains: "The threatening sky, the suggestion of a riverbank where the body will be thrown, and the desolate surrounding space all contribute to the menacing nature of the scene. . . . The sweeping movement of the male murderer, obvious in his jacket and legs, conveys the power of the moment."[19]

Even the portraits Cézanne painted at the time were harsh and dramatic. His *Portrait of Anthony Valabrègue* (1869–1870) is an example. In it, Valabrègue, a poet from Aix, is shown seated with a ferocious look in his eyes and his fists tightly clenched as if at any moment he will erupt in a fit of rage. Valabrègue's clothes are dark. So is the background. The heavy layers of paint show evidence of Cézanne's powerful emotions.

# The Salon

Cézanne submitted his portrait of Valabrègue to the Salon. The Salon was a vast annual or semiannual art exhibit that was controlled by the Academy of Fine Arts. It was attended by artists, art critics, the press, and art buyers from all over the world. Every artist wanted to exhibit there. There were few art dealers or galleries at the time. Practically the only way for artists to exhibit their work on a large scale, become well-known, and

# THE ÉCOLE DES BEAUX-ARTS

*Had Cézanne been accepted in the École des Beaux-Arts, his style of painting and the course of his career might have been quite different. In her book* The Private Lives of the Impressionists, *author Sue Roe describes the school:*

The Ecole des Beaux-Arts was an imposing institution on the Rue Bonaparte [Bonaparte Street]. . . . The Ecole, originally founded in 1684, consisted . . . of vast studios built round a series of leafy court-yards and cloisters. Its long corridors were littered with classical stat-ues . . . the walls decorated with friezes. . . . Inscribed around the ceiling in gold were the names of all the great masters: Holbein, Dürer, Rembrandt, Van Dyck, Velásquez. A central part of the curriculum was . . . copying of the Old Masters in the galleries of the Louvre. Students . . . received strict academic, classical training, which consisted of copying from the antique, learning anatomy by sketching from corpses . . . and learning to paint elevating religious and mythological subjects. On Monday mornings, the rue Bonaparte was crowded with models, already in costume (soldiers, shepherdesses), hoping to be picked for work. The teaching at the Ecole perpetuated the taste exemplified by the annual Salon exhibitions, and the goal . . . was to exhibit there.

Sue Roe. *The Private Lives of the Impressionists.* New York: HarperCollins, 2006, p. 8.

sell paintings was to participate in the annual Salon exhibition. Acceptance was so vital to success that some rejected artists committed suicide. Artist and art historian Jim Lane explains:

As painters today, we have no dominant art institu-tion to compare to the French Académie des Beaux-arts [Academy of Fine Arts], nor single, overriding "art contest" to compare with the Academy's annual Salons. . . . I guess about the only thing we have today to compare with this phenomena is the hullabaloo that goes on in Hollywood . . . when the Academy of Motion Picture Arts and Sciences nominates and then chooses Oscar winners. In a very real sense, the Salon shows were the Academy Awards of French painting with often just as much riding on a work being selected [for the exhibit] as is the case today with the similarly designated gold statuette.[20]

# Painted with a Pistol

It was not easy for even the most gifted artists to gain a place in the Salon. The Salon jury had rigid standards. Artwork that did not conform to their traditionalist rules was mocked and rejected. Making matters worse, the jury's opinion was repeated by art critics in newspapers, strongly influencing public sentiment. According to Lane: "It would be hard to imagine a more conservative gaggle of immobile, stodgy, establishment, stick-in-the-mud hacks bent upon cementing their high and mighty academic traditions in the minds of the public and artists alike, or a group of so-called 'art experts' in the press corps more dedicated to aiding and abetting the effort."[21]

*Portrait of Anthony Valabrègue*, with its thick, vigorous layers of paint, did not come close to the traditional, restrained artwork that the jury demanded. Valabrègue, who helped Cézanne load the painting into a wheelbarrow and push it through the streets of Paris, describes the jury's reaction to it: "A philistine [someone lacking in good taste] in the jury exclaimed on seeing my portrait that it was not only painted with a knife but with a pistol as well."[22]

This was not the first time, nor would it be the last, that Cézanne's work was dismissed by the jury. He unsuccessfully submitted paintings to the Salon every year from 1862 to 1882. Cézanne was not the only artist whose work was dismissed in this manner, although his work was rejected more frequently and more callously than most. Many artists, in hopes of gaining admission to the Salon, took pains to submit their least innovative works. Some created special formal works that followed old-fashioned artistic principles on

*Portrait of Anthony Valabrègue* (1866) is one of several of Cézanne's paintings rejected by the Salon jury.

composition, perspective, line, and color just to suit the jury. Cézanne refused to do this. In fact, he seemed to take pleasure in shocking the Salon jury.

# Salon des Refusés

Some years, the jury was more lenient about accepting the work of new artists, especially if they tailored their submissions to the jury's standards. Other years, the jury's prejudice against anything that departed in even the slightest way from the strict Neoclassical style was more severe. For instance, in 1863 the jury rejected 60 percent of the five thousand paintings submitted to the Salon. Among the rejected works were paintings by Cézanne, Édouard Manet, Camille Pissarro, and James Whistler, all artists who would someday be considered great masters. The rejected artists protested the obvious bias of the jury. Their outcry drew so much attention that France's Emperor Napoleon III interfered, permitting a second exhibit for the rejected work to be set up alongside the Salon. It would become known as the Salon des Refusés (the Salon of the Rejected).

Exhibiting in the Salon des Refusés was voluntary, and many artists withdrew their work in fear of angering the Academy members. More than three hundred artists, however, did participate. Cézanne was among them, although there is no record of what he exhibited.

The controversy surrounding the exhibition brought thousands of people to the Salon des Refusés, most of whom came to gawk and laugh at the paintings. One painting, *Luncheon on the Grass* by Manet, caused an uproar. It is a large realistic style work, which depicts a nude woman picnicking with two fully clothed men. In the background is another woman wearing little clothing about to go swimming. The depiction of the women, who are presumably prostitutes, repulsed the art establishment and the public. Manet's use of color was also shocking. At the time, artists used brown or black paint to depict shadows; they separated light-colored areas with areas of dark, and they used transitional tones to separate intense colors. Instead of painting

dark shadows, Manet used greens, yellows, and blues to depict reflected light. He also placed intense colors and light and dark colors beside each other. The painting's brightness appalled exhibition-goers. "Critics and the public, accustomed to pictures in which dull brown half-tones predominated, were nearly blinded by what seemed to them the crudity, the rank vulgarity, of so much intense color,"[23] Gerstle Mack explains. Cézanne, on the other hand, was inspired and delighted by the painting and Manet's use of color. It would have a lasting influence on his work.

*Luncheon on the Grass* (1863) by Édouard Manet was a big attraction at the Salon of the Rejected and a lasting influence on Cézanne's work.

## A Group of Rebels

The Salon des Refusés brought France's innovative young artists together. This group, which became known as the Batignolles

Group, included Édouard Manet, Claude Monet, Alfred Sisley, Edgar Degas, Pierre-Auguste Renoir, Camille Pissarro, Jean-Baptiste Antoine Guillemet, Frédéric Bazille, Henri Fantin-Latour, and Armand Guillaumin. Under the leadership of Manet, they met frequently in the Café Guerbois on the Rue de Batignolles (Batignolles Street), where they discussed painting and supported each other in their rebellion against the art establishment. They were particularly concerned with new theories on the depiction of light, shadow, and the use of color. They advocated painting *en plein air*, or outdoors, where the light was better and the colors richer. They dismissed overly romantic, emotional, classical, or historical work.

Cézanne attended many of these get-togethers. He usually said little unless something was said that he disagreed with. At such times, he flew into a rage and stormed out. Some of the group considered him a madman. Others like Pissarro, Monet, and Renoir befriended him. They respected Cézanne's talent. They defended and supported him, and would do so for years to come.

These three men would become the leaders of the Impressionist art movement. The Impressionists were concerned with depicting the ever-changing effects of light and color on the world around them. They painted outdoors and used short, feathery brushstrokes to gain the bright, clear effect or impression they desired. Cézanne found their ideas very interesting.

# A Decade of Work

The influence of the other artists began to appear in Cézanne's work. He spent much of the 1860s shuttling between Paris and Aix. He had not yet developed a distinct painting style, and he still tended to pile on thick layers of paint with his palette knife or glob it on with his brush. However, under the influence of Manet and the artists of the Batignolles, his work was changing. He started painting landscapes outdoors, most of which portrayed the gardens of Jas de Bouffan. Also, he experi-

ACHILLE EMPERAIRE PEINTRE

*Portrait of the Painter Achille Emperaire* (1868) is an example of Cézanne's experimentation with color.

mented with color. For example, in his *Portrait of the Painter Achille Emperaire* (1867–1868), Cézanne depicts his friend, the dwarf artist Emperaire, wearing a rich blue dressing gown over purple pants with a bright red scarf around his neck and red slippers on his feet. The small artist is seated in the same chair that appears in Cézanne's *The Artist's Father, Reading L'Evénement*. In the earlier painting, the flowery pattern on the chair is blurred and practically colorless. In the *Portrait of the Painter Achille Emperaire* the pattern is clear, precise, and colorful. It is in marked contrast to the pale chair of the earlier painting.

The painting, in its use of contrasting colors, its lack of prettiness, its choice of a dwarf as a subject, and the dignity and respect it bestows upon the dwarf, was bolder and more modern than the work of any other artist of the time. Cézanne submitted it, along with a painting of a nude woman, which has since been lost, to the Salon in 1870. As usual, both were rejected. Reporting on the entries, an art critic published a scathing attack on Cézanne's work. It was illustrated with a grotesque caricature of Cézanne in which he looked like a lunatic. Cézanne responded to the critic's attack defiantly: "I paint how I feel—and I have very strong feelings. . . . I take risks. I have the courage to stand by my opinions—and he who laughs last, laughs longest."[24]

Despite Cézanne's protest, such attacks would continue for most of his life. It took decades before he got the last laugh.

## Hortense Fiquet

Other things were also changing in Cézanne's life. In 1869 he began a relationship with a nineteen-year-old painter's model named Hortense Fiquet. She became Cézanne's mistress, bore him a son named Paul after his father, and became his wife in 1886.

Cézanne and Hortense spent a good part of their lives apart. Hortense preferred Paris to Aix. Although sometimes she and young Paul followed Cézanne to Aix, most of the time

*Opposite page:* Hortense Fiquet had to sit motionless for hours while Cézanne painted her for *Madame Cézanne in a Red Armchair* (1877).

they remained in Paris. This arrangement suited Cézanne, who did not enjoy spending extended periods of time with anyone and needed quiet and solitude to work. It also made it easier for Cézanne to keep the existence of his little family a secret from his father, who, the artist feared, would not approve of it. He did, however, tell his mother and his friends.

Hortense was not interested in art, and she had no idea of the importance of Cézanne's work. But she posed for him frequently and was the subject of forty-four paintings. In the earliest, she is portrayed as a plain young woman with dark hair and eyes and an angular face and figure. Later portraits show her aging. She appears thicker and more matronly. In all the paintings, she appears serene and emotionless. In reality she was a very talkative, lively woman. But she was able to sit without moving or talking for hours and felt it was her duty to pose for Cézanne. In this way, she contributed to his artwork.

## Sitting Out the War

In July 1870, France declared war on Prussia and other states in present-day Germany, beginning what was called the Franco-Prussian War. All able-bodied French men were expected to serve in the military. Cézanne had no interest in world affairs and no desire to take part in the war. In an effort to avoid being called up, he fled with Hortense to L'Estaque, a French fishing village 5 miles (8km) north of Marseille and 18 miles (29km) south of Aix where he was unlikely to be found by the draft board. Cézanne was enchanted by the rocky Mediterranean landscape and painted furiously. As his friends in Paris advocated, he worked outdoors and he tried to paint what he saw rather than what he imagined. But, as with his earlier work, he could not keep his emotions or his sense of drama out of his work. Also, he still used too much black paint.

His painting *Snow Thaw in L'Estaque* (1870) is an example of how Cézanne's effort to innovate mixed with his old style. The snow scene, with its steep snow-covered hillside, wind-bent trees, and red-roofed houses, is real. However, the thick layers

of paint, the gloomy colors of the leaden sky, the threat of an avalanche on the steep hill, and the unsteadiness of the twisted trees fill the scene with drama and despair. According to author and art historian Ulrike Becks-Malorny, "Cézanne's passionate temperament was still causing him problems, and his technique did not enable him to depict what he saw in nature with sufficient detachment and rigor."[25]

In *Snow Thaw in L'Estaque* (1870), Cézanne shows innovation mixed with his old style.

## Cézanne and Pissarro

Cézanne knew he needed help to improve his painting technique. When the war ended, he and Hortense returned to Paris where their son was born. It was not long before the city's hustle and bustle disturbed Cézanne. So Cézanne moved his family

# CAMILLE PISSARRO

Camille Pissarro was Cézanne's mentor and longtime friend. He was a kindly man who struggled financially throughout his life.

Pissarro (1830–1903) was born in St. Thomas, Virgin Islands. It was here that he began painting outdoors. In 1855, he moved to Paris where he was mentored by Camille Corot (1796–1875), a landscape artist who used clear, clean colors.

Focusing on the effects of light falling on objects in his paintings, Pissarro became a leader of the Impressionist movement. He painted in the Impressionist style until 1884, when he met Georges Seurat. For a time, Pissarro adopted Seurat's pointillist painting style. It involved applying small dots of contrasting colors to the canvas, which the eye perceived as a single color. Pissarro eventually found this method of painting too restrictive. Towards the end of his life, he turned his attention to painting Parisian street scenes in the style of his early Impressionistic work. In 1903, two of his paintings were hung in the Louvre.

In his role as a leader of the Impressionist movement, in his unfaltering opposition to the art establishment, and in his influence over Cézanne, Pissarro made a lasting impact on the history of art.

to Auvers. It was a picturesque village on the banks of the Oise River about 20 miles (32km) from Paris, not far from the home of Camille Pissarro, who would act as Cézanne's mentor.

Pissarro was nine years older than Cézanne. He was one of the first artists to paint *en plein air* and was a leader of the developing Impressionist movement. As a Jew from the West Indies, he, like Cézanne, was an outsider in Parisian society. His modest, patient nature and his belief in Cézanne's talent made him a perfect teacher for Cézanne. For two years, from 1872–1874, the two painted together in Auvers and in the nearby village of Pontoise.

One of the first things Pissarro did was encourage Cézanne to ignore all rules and paint directly from nature without adding anything from his own imagination. "Rely on your own personal style," he advised Cézanne. "Don't bother trying to look for something new. You won't find novelty in the subject matter, but in the way you express it."[26]

He also counseled Cézanne to stop using dark colors in his work and to discard his black paint entirely. "Only paint with three primary colors [red, yellow, and blue] and their derivatives," he advised. "Apply color everywhere and observe the tonal values closely in relation to the surroundings. Paint with small brushstrokes and try to record your observations immediately. The eyes must not concentrate on a specific point but should absorb everything and in doing so note the reflections of colors on their surroundings."[27]

Working with Pissarro, Cézanne gained more confidence. His work became lighter and brighter. He avoided large dark areas and he experimented with short, relaxed brushstrokes, but did not give up his palette knife entirely. He became enamored with painting outdoors and less and less interested in creating imaginary scenes. During the two years he spent with Pissarro, the major portion of his work was landscapes. According to art critic Jerry Saltz, "It was Pissarro who pulled Cézanne toward nature, away from expressionist painting, the palette knife excesses . . . and what art historian Roger Fry called 'artistic madness.' Cézanne needed Pissarro's restraint."[28]

By 1874, Cézanne had mastered the technique of the Impressionists, but he did not adopt it completely. Though Pissarro and Cézanne often painted the same subject, there were significant differences in their work. For instance, in 1871 Pissarro painted *Louveciennes*, a delightful scene of a small village in autumn. Author Leo J. O'Donovan describes the painting as a "gray, silver, and gold landscape subtly ordered into the foreground with a mother and child on a bending road, the

village velvet in the middle distance and the sky beyond a pearly pale blue."[29] Cézanne borrowed the painting and copied it in 1872. Although he was trying to duplicate the painting, in his version the colors are less subdued and the shapes are simplified.

When Cézanne was not trying to replicate Pissarro's work, there were even greater differences. Cézanne's *The House of the Hanged Man, Auvers-sur-Oise* (1873), which is considered by many his greatest Impressionist work, and Pissarro's *The Conversation, chemin du chou, Pontoise* (1874) are good examples.

Both paintings portray the same steep-roofed house set beside a winding road with a village in the background. Pissarro's painting is more polished and tamer than Cézanne's. In Pissarro's picture, people stroll along the road, welcoming the viewer into the scene. The light is milky and summery and the colors are harmonious blends of greens, grays, and blues. The overall effect is peaceful. Cézanne's depiction is wilder and less welcoming. It is angular with many overlapping planes. There are no people in the scene, and the house seems to be abandoned. It blends in with the surrounding countryside, almost as if it is part of it. The colors are not as pretty as those in Pissarro's painting, but they are closer to nature.

As time went on, the differences in the two men's work grew. Under the influence of Pissarro, Cézanne's work was changing and maturing. In the coming years Cézanne would combine what he learned from Pissarro with his own views of art, blazing a new path that was often misunderstood.

# 3

# "I Want to Make of Impressionism Something Solid and Durable"

The two years Paul Cézanne spent in Auvers were happy ones. He completed twenty-five paintings, considerably more than his usual output. The number suggests he was pleased with the results and destroyed fewer paintings than usual. Cézanne learned a lot from Pissarro and would always be grateful to him. "Pissarro," he told archaeologist Jules Borely in 1902, "was like a father to me. You could always ask him questions; he was something like the good God."[30] Yet once Cézanne mastered the painting methods of Pissarro and the Impressionists, he was driven to go beyond them.

## The Salon of Independent Artists

After the Salon des Refusés and the uproar it caused, the Salon jury made an effort to show more of the work of the young artists (with the exception of Cézanne, whose work was considered too radical) who would soon become known as Impressionists. Admittedly, their work was usually hung in inconspicuous corners or skyed—hung so high up that it could barely be seen—

but it still was shown. By 1870, the Impressionist style of outdoor painting, with its emphasis on clear colors, light tones, and shimmering shadows, was beginning to gain supporters among a small number of French art collectors. Threatened by this, in 1872 and 1873 the Salon jury banned work by the young artists from the Salon. In response, in 1874, twenty nontraditional artists, led by Pissarro, formed the Society of Painters, Sculptors, and Engravers with the intent of sponsoring their own exhibit financed by the artists.

The exhibit, which was held in 1874, featured the works of thirty artists, including Pissarro, Monet, Renoir, Sisley,

Cézanne's *A Modern Olympia* (1873–1874) was met with ridicule and derision. A painting on the same subject by Manet had caused a scandal about a decade earlier.

Guillaumin, Berthe Morisot, Degas, and Cézanne. Manet was sympathetic to the artists, but chose not to take part.

The exhibit opened in April and lasted one month. Approximately thirty-five hundred people, including at least fifty art critics, attended. Their reaction to the new style of painting was not what the artists hoped for. Cézanne's work, especially, was met with outrage and laughter. He exhibited three paintings. Two were landscapes—*The House of the Hanged Man, Auvers-sur-Oise* and *Landscape in Auvers* (1873). The third was *A Modern Olympia* (1873–1874). Cézanne painted it in an act of defiance against the response to Manet's *Olympia*, a painting of a naked prostitute, which caused a scandal when it was exhibited in the Salon of 1865. Cézanne's version was more daring than Manet's. His painting depicts a naked woman partially crouching, partially reclining on a sofa. A black male servant is fanning her, while a man who resembles Cézanne stares at her. The painting's luminous colors, bold theme, and erotic character unleashed a flood of ridicule from the press and the public. In the journal *L'artiste*, art critic Marc de Montifaud wrote: "Like a voluptuous vision, this artificial corner of paradise has left even the most courageous gasping for breath. . . . Mr. Cézanne . . . gives the impression of being a sort of madman, painting in a state of delirium tremens [a "shaking frenzy" caused by alcohol withdrawal]."[31]

His landscapes were not treated any better. Montifaud wrote in the same article, "When it comes to landscapes, Monsieur Cézanne will permit us to pass in silence over his. . . . We confess that they are more than we can swallow."[32]

Not everyone attending the exhibit was scornful of Cézanne's work. Count Doria, a collector of contemporary art, bought *The House of the Hanged Man, Auvers-sur-Oise* for 300 francs ($60). Also, Doctor Paul-Fernand Gachet, an art collector with unconventional taste who befriended Cézanne in Auvers, purchased *A Modern Olympia*.

Even with these two sales, Cézanne did not make enough money to pay for his share of the exhibit's cost and was forced

# ÉDOUARD MANET

**É**douard Manet was not an Impressionist, but his work inspired the Impressionists. He was a charming and handsome man. Although he was considered by some to be unconventional, he actually led a typical middle-class life. In fact, the uproar that some of his work caused in the art world upset him greatly. He studied classical art, and put great value on Salon acceptance. Indeed, his most controversial work, *Luncheon on the Grass* (1863), was based on an engraving by Raphael, and *Olympia* (1863) was based on Titian's *Venus of Urbino*.

Manet modernized classical subjects. He was inspired by Courbet and the realistic school of painting and believed that art should reflect contemporary life. He often portrayed beggars, prostitutes, and middle-class life in his work. The realness of his work, however, shocked the art establishment. At the same time, his use of color fascinated artists like Cézanne, Renoir, and Monet. Furthermore, his insistence on painting his unique vision of the world inspired the Impressionists to break free from the constraints of the traditional art establishment and pursue their own artistic visions. He died in Paris, France, on April 30, 1883.

to borrow from his father. The other artists, too, sold paintings. But, in general, the exhibit was more a source of amusement for the public than a source of recognition or income for the artists. One thing the exhibit did was give the nontraditional artists' painting style a name: Impressionism. While the term is used today, it was not widely used until 1874. The name came from a mocking attack in the press on *Impression, Sunrise*, a landscape by Claude Monet. It soon caught on as a label for the whole art movement.

# A Major Turning Point

Despite the criticism and financial loss, the exhibit had a posi-
tive impact on how Cézanne felt about his artistic abilities. The
new techniques he had learned from Pissarro, the sale of his
paintings, and the support of art collectors like Gachet and
Victor Chocquet, a minor government official who was so taken
with Cézanne's work that he became one of the artist's greatest
defenders, gave him more confidence. Also, the praise of people
he respected such as Renoir, who said of Cézanne, "He can't put
two strokes of color on a canvas without it already being very
good,"[33] made Cézanne increasingly indifferent to public opinion.

This was a turning point in Cézanne's life. Although he
continued to struggle with his emotions and often be incredibly
frustrated with his work, he never again doubted the importance
of what he was doing. He believed that someday his work would
be recognized. He knew he might not live to see this happen,
but he hoped that would not be the case. This faith gave him the
courage to persevere despite what the press or the public thought.
A letter that he wrote to his mother in 1874 shows his newfound
confidence and growing indifference to public opinion:

> I am beginning to consider myself stronger than those
> all around me, and you know the good opinion I have
> of myself has only been reached after serious consid-
> eration. I have to work all the time, but not to achieve
> that final perfection, which earns the admiration of
> imbeciles—and this thing which is commonly so
> appreciated so much is merely the effect of craftsman-
> ship and renders all work resulting from it inartistic
> and common. I must strive after perfection only for the
> satisfaction of becoming truer and wiser.[34]

# A Secret Life

After the exhibit, Cézanne returned to Aix. For the next two
years, he spent most of his time there or in L'Estaque. Hortense

and little Paul remained in Paris. Hortense preferred Parisian life. Plus, remaining far away from Aix made it easier for Cézanne to hide his little family's existence from his father, whom Cézanne feared would cut off his allowance if he knew about Cézanne's mistress and son.

Although Cézanne was approaching his thirty-fifth birthday, he still depended on his father for money. Cézanne's allowance, most of which he used to support Hortense and little Paul, came with strings attached. Louis-Auguste treated the artist like a child. He kept track of Cézanne's whereabouts, expected him home for dinner every night when he was in Aix, and even opened his mail. The latter made it impossible for Cézanne to communicate with his family. He worried about young Paul, to whom he was very devoted. Cézanne had to depend on Pissarro and Zola to check on his family, then send him news of them in letters without mentioning Hortense's or young Paul's names or their relationship to Cézanne. Cézanne did not like living a double life. But the thought of losing his allowance, and therefore, the freedom to paint trumped his desire to reveal his secret.

## The Sea at L'Estaque

During these two years, Cézanne worked tirelessly. He painted outdoors as much as possible. He completed several portraits of his sisters and uncle, several studies of nude bathers, a number of landscapes of the gardens of Jas de Bouffant, and seascapes of L'Estaque. In the six years since he had painted the somber *Snow Thaw in L'Estaque*, his style had changed dramatically. The drab colors, dramatic touches, and stark contrasts of the earlier painting were gone. *The Sea at L'Estaque* (1876) is a good example of how his work had matured. It is a tranquil, brightly colored seascape that depicts exactly what Cézanne saw without a trace of violence, foreboding, or wild emotions. According to Ulrike Becks-Malorny:

> The painting is carefully structured, with the strong colors—the terracotta roof tiles, the green foliage, the

blue surface of the water—covering the surface of the canvas with great intensity. There is no definable lighting; only the red chimney is glowing in the low sun. It is not the light which breaks up the outlines of the forms. . . . Instead of light, the forms are defined by . . . color. It is color which determines the nature of objects and both brings them nearer to the viewer and places them at an immeasurable distance away. We can see from the painting that Cézanne has become a closer observer of nature, and nothing has been added purely for effect.[35]

Cézanne's style changed dramatically with his brightly colored painting *The Sea at L'Estaque.*

**"I Want to Make of Impressionism Something Solid and Durable"** 55

# KIND WORDS

*The general reaction to the paintings Cézanne exhibited at the Third Impressionist Exhibition in 1877 was quite negative. Yet a few art critics, writing for tiny radical publications that were seen by few people, were more enthusiastic. This is what one of those critics, Georges Rivière, wrote:*

The most attacked and maligned by press and public alike over the last fifteen years is M[onsieur] Cézanne. . . . M. Cézanne is a painter and a great painter. Those who have never held a brush or a pencil have said he doesn't know how to draw, and they've reproached him for "imperfections" that are nothing other than refinements procured through immense skill.

I know well that, despite everything, M. Cézanne cannot have success like that obtained by fashionable painters. . . . However, M. Cézanne's painting has the inexpressible charm of biblical or Greek antiquity, the movements of the figures are simple and grand like those of ancient sculpture, the landscapes have an imposing majesty, and his still lifes so beautiful, so precise in his tonal relationships, have a certain solemnity in their truth. All the artist's pictures are moving because he himself experiences a violent emotion before nature that skill transfers to the canvas.

Quoted in Francoise Cachin, Isabelle Cahn, Walter Feilchenfeldt, Henri Loyrette, Joseph J. Rishel. *Cézanne.* New York: Harry N. Abrams, 1996, p. 26.

## A Final Exhibit

In 1876, while Cézanne was working in L'Estaque, the Impressionists held a second exhibit. Cézanne was invited to exhibit, but he declined. It is likely he was still paying his father back for the cost of the first exhibit, and did not want to go further in debt. He did, however, participate in the Third Impressionist Exhibition in 1877. This would be the last time Cézanne would exhibit his work for many years.

Only eighteen artists showed their work at the exhibit, and it would be the last time that they all exhibited together. Many art historians consider these eighteen artists to be the most important artists of the time. The members of the group who would become the most famous included Cézanne, Pissarro, Monet, Renoir, Morisot, Sisley, and Degas.

The exhibit was held in a large empty house. Pissarro, Renoir, and Monet were in charge of the placement of the pictures. They gave the finest position in the show to Cézanne. These men genuinely respected Cézanne's work, and felt that his treatment by the press, public, and the art establishment was undeserved. They hoped that giving his paintings a place of honor might favorably influence the opinion of exhibition-goers. Unfortunately, this was not the case.

Cézanne exhibited sixteen paintings. Among the group were landscapes, still lifes, portraits, and a study of bathers. Throughout his life, Cézanne would paint about two hundred studies of bathers. His interest in this theme started with "The Inseparables" and continued until his death. Cézanne painted the landscapes for his bather studies directly from nature and from the naked figures from early drawings he had made at the Académie Suisse or from works in the Louvre. His bather studies changed over time as his work became more abstract. The six female figures in the study that he showed at the 1877 exhibit are fairly realistic, but they lack individuality or facial features. The landscape is bright and vibrant. The bathers' flesh is dotted with blues and greens reflected off the water. Depicting the bathers' skin in this way, rather than entirely in traditional pink, shocked the public, who crowded around the painting to gape and laugh.

Cézanne's *Portrait of Victor Chocquet* (1876–1877) also drew throngs of disdainful viewers. Today most people would realize that the blue-green tones in Chocquet's beard and hair and the reds and yellows in his skin are reflections cast by light. But in

58　Paul Cézanne

1877, such use of color was considered crazy. In response to the painting, one journalist mockingly warned pregnant exhibition-goers not to look at the painting too long, lest the yellow tones give their infants yellow fever. "Opinion," Mack explains, "was divided on whether [Cézanne] was a madman or a monster. . . . The enormous vitality of his works, the solidity and depth of his painting, the complete absence of prettiness in his treatment of his subjects, bewildered and shocked even those who had begun to accept, however hesitatingly, the more subdued, less forceful canvases of his associates."[36]

# Bad Times

After the exhibit, Cézanne returned to Aix, where he lived in Jas de Bouffan with his parents and sisters. He divided much of his time between Aix and L'Estaque. He moved Hortense and little Paul to Marseilles. It was close enough to L'Estaque that Cézanne could visit them frequently, but far enough from Aix to keep them hidden from Cézanne's father. But in 1878, Cézanne's secret came out. Louis-Auguste opened a letter to Cézanne from Chocquet, in which Chocquet inadvertently mentioned Hortense and young Paul. Shortly thereafter Louis-Auguste spied his son coming out of a toy shop carrying a wooden rocking horse and other toys. Next, he had his son followed. It was not long before Louis-Auguste knew the truth. When Louis-Auguste confronted Cézanne, Cézanne, not wanting to anger his father, denied the existence of his family. Calling Cézanne's bluff, the older man cut the artist's allowance in half, telling his son that the smaller sum was enough to support a lone man without a family. It was not enough, especially since young Paul had caught an illness and was in need of a doctor. Soon Cézanne was struggling. He considered looking for a job in an office, which meant he would no longer be able to devote himself to painting. He asked Zola to help him find work. Instead, Zola, who was now a wealthy and successful writer, lent Cézanne enough money to make up the deficit. Zola supplemented Cézanne's income for six months. Then, without

*Opposite page:* The tones Cézanne used for the skin and hair color in *Portrait of Victor Chocquet* (1876–1877) were considered shocking at the time.

Cézanne painted *L'Estaque, View of the Bay of Marseilles* in 1878–1879. His wife and son lived in Marseilles while Cézanne lived in L'Estaque so that he could visit them more easily.

explanation, Louis-Auguste raised Cézanne's allowance, and never cut it down again. It is not known what changed the older man's mind, but it is likely that Cézanne's mother, who always supported her son, had a hand in it.

## Capturing Both Light and Substance to Reveal the "Essence"

With a raise in his allowance, Cézanne was able to pursue his art and care for his family. Between 1878 and 1882, he moved back and forth between the outskirts of Paris, Aix, and L'Estaque. The Impressionists continued to have exhibitions from 1879 to 1882 and again in 1886. They invited Cézanne to participate, but after 1877 Cézanne did not exhibit with them again. He kept in touch with Pissarro, Renoir, and Monet, and admired their work all his life. "Pissarro," he told Aix poet Joachim Gasquet years later, "had an enormous influence on me. . . . It's he who was really the first Impressionist. . . . Renoir is skillful. . . . Monet is an eye, the most prodigious [exceptional] eye in the history of painters. . . . [His work] will endure. . . . He'll be in the Louvre."[37]

Yet, despite his admiration for the Impressionists' work, Cézanne no longer felt he was part of the group. His work was straying further and further from their style. Impressionism was concerned with painting the effects of light on objects during a moment in time at the expense of depth, solidity, and form. Cézanne did not want to capture just the momentary effects of light or the surface appearance of light on an object. He wanted to capture the effects of light, as well as the solid permanent form beneath the surface or what he called the "essence" of the object. "Nature," he said, "is more depth than surface."[38]

Art critic Peter Schjeldahl explains:

Cézanne worked through Impressionism and beyond Impressionism, dissatisfied with a style that sacrificed physical structure for retinal [visual] sensation. He declared, "I want to make of Impressionism something solid and durable, like the art of the museums." In struggling stages he did so, merging light and substance—Impressionist immediacy and the density of matter.[39]

Cézanne felt the only way to achieve his goal was by painstakingly studying his subject before ever laying brush to canvas. He could spend weeks analyzing a scene before he started work. "Everything we see is fleeting," he told Gasquet:

Nature is always the same, but nothing about her that we see endures. Our art must convey a glimmer of her endurance with the elements, the appearance of all her changes. It must give her a sense of eternity. . . . So I join her . . . I pick her tonalities, her colors, her nuances from the left, from the right, here, there, everywhere. I fix them. I bring them together. They form lines. They become objects, rocks, trees. . . . They take on volume. They have color values. . . . Nature doesn't waver. . . . But if I have the least distraction, the slightest lapse, if I interpret too much one day . . . then bang! All is lost.[40]

# Entering the Salon through the Back Door

Even though Cézanne did not exhibit with the Impressionists after 1877, he continued to send an entry to the Salon each year. He anticipated being rejected, and would probably have been shocked if his paintings were accepted. It is unknown why he kept submitting his work. He may have done so to prove to those who disdained his work that he could obtain a place in the official exhibition. Or he may have done so in hopes of gaining recognition and increased sales. No matter his reason, it is clear that the regular rejection hurt him. He described the experience in a letter to Pissarro as "undergoing the dry guillotine."[41]

In 1882, artist Jean-Baptiste Antoine Guillemet gained a place on the Salon's jury. Guillemet had been a part of the Batignolles Group and attended the Académie Suisse with Cézanne. He began his art career as a rebel, but over the years his painting style had become more and more traditional. Yet he recognized Cézanne's talent and felt Cézanne had been mistreated by the art establishment. In 1882, each member of the jury was allowed to select the work of one of their art students to exhibit in the Salon without a challenge from other jurors. Although Cézanne was not Guillemet's student, Guillemet claimed he was. In this way, Cézanne was finally able to exhibit a painting in the Salon.

The painting received so little recognition that it is unknown what it was. The Salon catalog listed the work as *Portrait of*

*Opposite page: Cézanne painted Houses in Provence: The Riaux Valley Near L'Estaque in the 1880s. During this time, he did not receive the critical acclaim that he had dreamed of as a youth, but was developing a style that aimed to reproduce the essence of nature.*

*Monsieur L.A.* This might have been one of the many portraits Cézanne painted of his uncle Louis Aubert or his *The Artist's Father, Reading L'Evénement.* In any event, the painting was hung in so dark, obscure, and high a corner that it received no notice at all.

Disappointed with the event, Cézanne stopped submitting his paintings to the Salon. He resigned himself to obscurity, "to work in silence until the day when I shall feel able to defend in the theory the results of my efforts,"[42] he said at the time.

In the 1870s and early 1880s, Cézanne did not gain the acclaim or critical support he had dreamed about as a youth. He did have the support of friends and fellow artists who believed in his vision, however. Although it hurt him to be rejected by the art establishment, he had more important things on his mind. In his attempts to reproduce the essence of nature, he was creating a new type of art. That was what mattered to him most. In his words:

> The goal of the artist is to work without worrying about anyone and to become stronger. . . . The artist must shun the opinions not based on the intelligent observation of essentials. He must . . . dedicate himself totally to the study of nature and try to produce painting which enlightens. Conversations about art are useless. Work, which brings about progress in one's art, is sufficient consolation for being misunderstood by fools.[43]

# "I Will Astonish Paris with an Apple"

Cézanne returned to Aix in 1882. For the next three years, he divided his time between Aix and L'Estaque. He went to Paris in 1883 to attend Édouard Manet's funeral, which was also attended by Renoir, Pissarro, Monet, and Zola. Cézanne did not stay and visit with his friends. Instead, he hurried back to L'Estaque to paint. He was obsessed with truly seeing and capturing the essence of nature. Cézanne saw nature in everything from fields, to people, to fruit. He painted landscapes, portraits, and still lifes with equal concentration.

## Creating a New Way to Portray Space

Cézanne found inspiration in the scenery around L'Estaque. As he wrote to Zola in 1883:

> I've rented a little house with a garden in L'Estaque just above the train station and at the foot of the hill, where behind me rise the rocks and pines. I keep myself busy painting. . . . I have some beautiful viewpoints here. . . .

*Rocks at L'Estaque* dates from 1879–1882. Cézanne's use of space is among his greatest contributions to modern art.

Climbing on the heights when the sun is setting, one has a glorious view of Marseille in the distance and the islands, the whole giving a very decorative effect in the evening light.[44]

In trying to capture the essence of what he saw, he faced many challenges. One of the greatest was how to represent three-dimensional objects on a flat canvas. Since the Renaissance in the 1400s, artists had accomplished this through two techniques—linear perspective and modelling, either individually or in combination. In modelling, artists portray an object's depth through light to dark shading. However, in carefully studying nature, Cézanne realized that not only do the light and dark tones on the surface of an object change as the object recedes, but the actual colors change, too. Viewing the brilliant sun, blue water, and vivid colors of L'Estaque made this clear to him. As he wrote Pissarro:

> I fancy the country where I am would suit you marvelously. . . . It is like a playing card. Red roofs against the blue sea. . . . It's olive trees and pines, which always keep their leaves. The sun here is so frightful that it seems to me that objects are silhouetted not only in white or black, but in blue, red, brown, violet. I could be wrong, but it seems to me that it is the opposite of modelling.[45]

Based on his realization, rather than depending on shading to suggest the solidness of objects, Cézanne used color. He developed his own system in which he applied thin glazes of color in layer upon layer of innumerable small brushstrokes. Each stroke was laid down meticulously in definite directions to render the solidity and shape of objects by means of color. He used cool colors like blue and green to make objects or planes recede and warm colors like yellow and red to make them stand out. According to Becks-Malorny, "He spoke of the particular ability of blue to give breadth and height to a space or, as he put it, 'to make the air tangible.'"[46] He used color to create areas of light and shadow, and he used contrasting colors to create the structure of his paintings. In this way, he was able to depict solidity and space without losing the sparkling light and color of the Impressionists.

Cézanne also did not think that portraying depth through linear perspective captured what he saw. By directing parallel lines towards the horizon, and depicting closer objects as larger in size and farther objects as smaller in size, artists use linear perspective to give the illusion of depth. Linear perspective makes a painting seem almost like a window looking out

# POSTIMPRESSIONISM

Cézanne moved beyond Impressionism in his artwork. Art historians classify Cézanne as both an Impressionist and a Postimpressionist. The Postimpressionists consist of a group of artists with diverse artistic styles who never worked together or considered themselves a collective group like the Impressionists did. Their work features innovative use of color and geometric shapes and distorted perspective. They sought to express emotions or permanence rather than transient impressions in their work.

Cézanne was the oldest of these artists, and his work inspired two other members of the group, Paul Gauguin (1848–1903) and Vincent van Gogh (1853–1890). Gauguin's work features solid, flat patches of color, clearly defined forms, and distorted perspective. He is best known for his paintings depicting life in Tahiti. Gauguin owned one of Cézanne's paintings, which he treasured. Cézanne did not like Gauguin or his work. He felt the younger artist was trying to steal his techniques.

Dutch artist Van Gogh was so inspired by Cézanne that he went to Provence to paint. Van Gogh's work features bright color, frantic lines, and distorted perspective. On viewing Van Gogh's work, Cézanne said that Van Gogh painted like a madman.

into the world. Starting in the 1850s, artists like Manet and the Impressionists began to think of their paintings as separate worlds in which space was depicted as a flat surface. Cézanne found this approach, too, incompatible with nature. He wanted to depict both flatness and solidity in his paintings. Since he saw things from many angles, with two eyes that moved and a head that turned, he wanted to portray multiple perspectives in his paintings, making some objects appear as if they were seen from above and others from the side, front, or back. To get the effect he wanted, Cézanne created a new way of depicting space that combined elements of linear perspective with the Impressionists' way of depicting space as a flat surface. Doing so somewhat distorted the size and shape of objects, which gave his paintings a modern look that had not been seen before. Artist Nancy Doyle explains:

> This combining caused his paintings to have both flatness and three-dimensional space; the forms have both volume AND flatness. This combination causes a certain tension in his work—which is so perfectly resolved that the tension provides movement, and his resolution of the tension provides an eternal harmony. This combining of two types of space also accounts for his distortions of objects and perspective; depicting the "correct" perspective would destroy the visual integrity of the flat pictorial surface.[47]

Many art historians say that Cézanne's method of depicting space is his greatest contribution to art and the biggest influence on twentieth-century modern art.

# Constructing a Painting

To portray this new type of space, Cézanne did not simply paint a picture. He constructed it, much like a sculptor builds a statue or an architect a building. First, he carefully analyzed the scene before him, whether it was a rural road, a bowl of fruit, or a person. Then he selected the most important part of the scene to paint. He called this the "motif." Before he laid brush to canvas, he considered the composition or arrangement of objects in his painting, the colors, the space, and viewing angles, and how each impacted the next. He rarely copied a scene and often enlarged objects that he felt were important and shrunk those that he thought were less significant. As a result, he distorted shape and perspective to suit his vision.

70    Paul Cézanne

Finally, once he planned his painting, he began to work. He did not draw on the canvas, but instead built his picture with color. Using thousands of small, elongated brushstrokes, he laid down thin layers of transparent, luminous color. He carefully considered the angle, color, spatial relationship, and artistic function of each brushstroke, and would destroy or discard a painting based on one or two awkward strokes. He often worked on a painting for years, touching and retouching it. According to Doyle:

> He simply wouldn't give up until either he felt the picture finally was perfectly unified and resolved, or that it would never be; in the latter case, he might destroy it or leave it in a field. His paintings are all more than the sum of their parts. He juggled all the variables of painting: each stroke had to carry its proper place, color, value, spatial relationship, drawing, and expressive function. . . . Each stroke played a crucial role in the visual structure of the painting, an almost god-like ambition; somewhat like having every word in a 1000-page novel be exactly, precisely the right word—without a single superfluous or uncomfortable fit. . . . Part of the power lies in the pictorial structure, which is the first time in painting that the visual structure, of a landscape or still life, is actually constructed on the canvas; it is the architecture, the skeleton that the colors hang on. . . . The beauty of the three-dimensional perfection is astounding.[48]

*Opposite page: Boy in a Red Waistcoat* (1888–1890) shows how perspective and color became important in Cézanne's paintings.

## Discarded Work

Cézanne spent almost every waking hour trying to capture nature. Yet once he was done with a painting, whether because he thought the work finished or because he was not satisfied with it, he had little use for it. He was known to leave his paintings, which he termed "experiments," behind as he moved from apartment to apartment, abandon them in the fields, shove them into a dark corner of his studio in Aix where they often became dirty or torn, trade them for food or services with merchants, or give them away to neighbors and friends. Zola, Pissarro, Monet, and Renoir all had Cézanne's work hanging in their homes. More than anyone, though, it was Julien Tanguy who kept Cézanne's work from being forgotten.

Tanguy was a Parisian paint merchant. Cézanne, Monet, Pissarro, and Renoir were among his regular customers. Tanguy regarded the artists as his friends. He gave them unlimited credit and often accepted seemingly unsalable paintings in exchange for paints. Over time, he accumulated a large collection of paintings, which he kept in a back room. In this way, Tanguy unwittingly rescued many of Cézanne's paintings from abandonment or destruction. Because Tanguy greatly admired Cézanne's work, he often showed it to his customers. For many years, Tanguy's shop was the only public place where Cézanne's work could be seen.

As the years went by, young artists like Vincent van Gogh, Paul Gauguin, and Émile Bernard saw Cézanne's work in Tanguy's shop and became inspired by it. According to Bernard, "This modest shop had considerable influence on the present generation. . . . Over a twenty-year period, the Cézannes burned with a contained fire, and all the artists and art lovers in Paris went to see them. To draw up the list of . . . visitors would be to write the history of current art."[49]

## A Turbulent Time

Cézanne's work consumed him until 1885, when he fell in love with an unknown woman whom he met in Aix. Little is known about the woman or the relationship. What is known is that the stress of the affair interfered with his ability to paint.

Hoping a change of scenery would calm him down, in June 1885 Cézanne went to stay with the Renoirs in a picturesque village on the Seine River north of Paris. He intended to spend the summer painting with his friend. But he was too upset to concentrate. After about a month, he abandoned his work in the

*Opposite page: Cézanne completed* The Pipe Smoker *in 1890.*

countryside and went to see Zola, hoping his old friend could advise him on his love life. Sadly, this would be the last time Cézanne and Zola would ever speak to each other. There is no record of what was said. But it appears that it helped Cézanne. Cézanne returned to Aix in mid-July. He feverishly resumed painting and never mentioned the mysterious woman again. In fact, in April 1886 he finally married Hortense.

A few months later, in October 1886, Cézanne's father died. He left Cézanne four hundred thousand francs, an amount equivalent to more than a million in today's U.S. dollars. Cézanne was now the head of the family and a rich man. Although he continued to live simply, the money provided him with security. He no longer worried about losing his allowance and giving up painting.

Cézanne completed *Paul Alexis (Secretary to Zola), Reading to Émile Zola* in 1870, when he and Zola were still close friends.

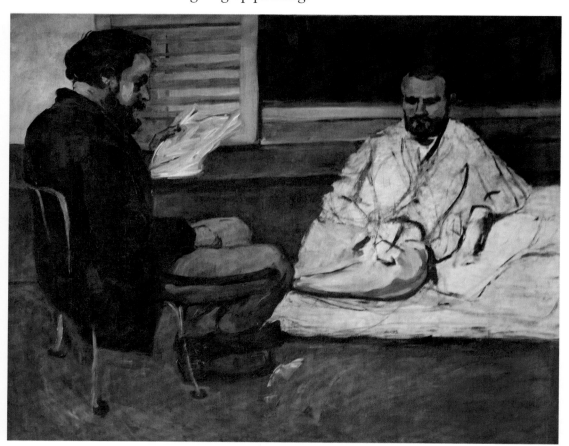

# A Friendship Ends

Besides losing his father in 1886, Cézanne lost his oldest and dearest friend, Émile Zola. In 1886, Zola's novel *L'Oeuvre* (*The Masterpiece*) was published. The main character in the book is a mad, unsuccessful artist named Claude Lantier, who seems to be based on Cézanne. Shunned by the art establishment and unable to transfer his artistic vision onto canvas, Lantier commits suicide.

Lantier's resemblance to Cézanne hurt the artist. It seemed to him that his best friend considered him a failure, and did not recognize the quality of his work. Cézanne sent Zola a terse note thanking him for the book and never communicated with him again. Zola tried to keep up with Cézanne through mutual friends, but Cézanne had nothing more to do with him. Yet Cézanne never stopped caring about his childhood friend. In 1902, when Cézanne heard of Zola's death, he burst into tears and locked himself in his studio to grieve.

# "You Must Sit Like an Apple"

Despite the upsets and turbulence in his life, Cézanne continued painting. Between his long and deliberate study of his subjects and his painstaking painting technique, his work progressed extremely slowly. Portraits were especially difficult. Posing for Cézanne was excruciating. Cézanne expected his subjects to sit for hours on end without moving. If they blinked an eye, or said a word, he would become enraged. "You must sit like an apple. Does an apple move?,"[50] he was known to scream.

Not surprisingly, it was difficult for Cézanne to get people to pose for him, which is why he painted so many self-portraits and portraits of Hortense. Those who did pose usually look quite somber. This is probably because they were so uncomfortable. In 1899, Cézanne painted a portrait of the art dealer Ambroise Vollard. Cézanne seated Vollard on an uncomfortable chair precariously perched on a rickety platform. Cézanne

*Opposite page:*
The subject sat
for Cézanne 115
times while the art-
ist painted *Portrait
of Ambroise Vollard*
(1899).

made Vollard sit for him one hundred and fifteen times. Each session lasted four hours without breaks. Any little movement on Vollard's part or sound from the street could enrage Cézanne. The weather, which affected the light, also caused the artist grief. Vollard described the torturous nature of these sittings:

> Whenever he began a sitting or took up his interrupted work, Cézanne, his brush raised, always looked at me with an unyielding fixed gaze. . . . Very few people have seen Cézanne paint. He could barely stand to be watched while he was at his easel. For those who had not seen him paint, it is difficult to imagine how slow and difficult this work was on some days. In my portrait, there are two little places on the hand where the canvas is unpainted. I drew this to his attention. . . . "Maybe tomorrow I'll find the right tone to cover those white patches. But please understand, Mr. Vollard, if I were to put just any color there at random, I would be forced to take my picture and leave!" And that prospect made me shudder.[51]

As a matter of fact, Cézanne never filled in the two white spots on Vollard's hands. Many of Cézanne's paintings have similar blank areas. Cézanne often put paintings aside, planning to go back and retouch them years later. Even so, he did not always find the color he was looking for. For this reason, a number of his paintings have small blank spots.

## "I Will Astonish Paris with an Apple"

Painting inanimate objects that could not move was less frustrating for the artist. Cézanne painted almost two hundred still lifes, returning often to the same subjects: fruit, onions, skulls, flowers, bottles, jars, pitchers, baskets, and a crumbled white tablecloth. Apples, especially, appear in many of his still lifes.

# GIVING LIFE TO INANIMATE OBJECTS

*It has often been said that Cézanne's portraits were essentially still-life paintings since he required that his subjects never move. On the other hand, Cézanne seems to give life to the inanimate objects in his still life paintings. In a 1912 essay, pioneer abstract artist Wassily Kandinsky (1866–1944) saw it this way:*

Cézanne made a living thing out of a teacup or, rather, in a teacup he realized the existence of something alive. He raised still life to the point where it ceased to be inanimate. He painted things as he painted human beings, because he was endowed with the gift of divining the eternal life in everything. He achieved expressive color and a form that harmonized this color with an almost mathematical abstraction. A man, a tree, an apple are not represented but used by Cézanne in building up a painterly thing called "a picture."

Quoted in Nicholas Wadley. *The Paintings of Cézanne*. New York: Mallard Press, 1989, p. 51.

"I will astonish Paris with an apple,"[52] Cézanne told art critic Gustave Geffroy in 1895, shortly before the artist's work was shown in that city.

Cézanne knew he would not astonish Paris with the subject, but rather with the way he used color, form, and multiple perspectives to depict the subject. Indeed, Cézanne's apples, and the still life paintings they appear in, are among his most celebrated works. Many art historians consider Cézanne to be the greatest painter of still lifes ever. Wrote journalist Thadée Natanson in 1895,

[Cézanne] can already lay claim to being the French school's new master of still life. Given the love with which he paints them and imbues them with all his gifts, he is and remains a painter of apples—apples that are smooth, round, fresh, ponderous, dazzling, of shifting color. . . . He has made apples his own. Through his magisterial [commanding] grasp they now belong to him. They are his, as much as any object belongs to its creator.[53]

Cézanne spent much time constructing his still-life motifs. He carefully selected and arranged the objects, balancing their colors, shapes, sizes, and spatial relationships. He wanted every part of his painting, including the background and tablecloth, to

Cézanne's depiction of depth and space is most noticeable in his still lifes, such as *Kitchen Table* (*Still life with basket*) (1888–1890).

be in harmony. He was not interested in creating a scene from daily life. Rather, he was concerned with capturing the shapes and colors of the objects and their relationship in space. These, he believed, were the essential forms of nature. Artist Louis Le Bail, who visited Cézanne's studio towards the end of Cézanne's life, describes the process: "The cloth was draped very slightly upon the table with innate taste; then Cézanne arranged the fruits, contrasting the tones of one against the other, making the complementaries vibrate, the greens against the reds, the yellows against the blues, tipping, turning, balancing the fruits as he wanted them to be, using coins . . . for the purpose. He brought to this task the greatest care."[54]

Once he had constructed his motif, Cézanne went on to build his painting. His new method of depicting depth and space is most apparent in his still lifes. For instance, in *The Kitchen Table* (*Still life with basket*) (1888–1890), Cézanne presents many points of view simultaneously. Most of the objects are seen from the front, but the ginger jar is viewed from above, and the fruit basket, next to the jar, is seen from the front and the side. The table appears to tilt forward, with one side lower than the other. The design makes viewers move their gaze in almost a zigzag fashion, which gives the picture great depth. According to modern artist Georges Braque, this type of perspective makes it seem "as if the artist were behind rather than in front of the canvas, pushing everything outwards."[55]

The unique shape and vibrant colors of each fruit, the way they seem to glow from within, the contrasting colors and planes, the way each object changes color depending on the position of its surface, and the way Cézanne uses layers of color rather than lines to depict form also add depth and solidity.

# Uneventful Exhibits

It took Cézanne just as long to paint a still life as a portrait or a landscape. Because fruit rotted and flowers withered before he finished a painting, he frequently used paper flowers and artificial fruit. His only concern was painting. He no longer

made any attempt to exhibit his work. However in 1889, Victor Chocquet managed to get Cézanne's painting *The House of the Hanged Man, Auvers-sur-Oise* exhibited at the World's Fair held in Paris. Chocquet owned an antique chair that the fair's conservative art committee wanted to display. Chocquet refused to loan the chair unless the committee exhibited *The House of the Hanged Man, Auvers-sur-Oise*, which Chocquet now owned. The committee agreed to the deal, but they hung the painting in the most inconspicuous place, where it drew almost no attention, which is what the art committee intended.

The indifference to the painting made Cézanne even less interested in showing his work when, in 1890, an independent group of Belgian artists invited Cézanne to take part in an exhibition in Brussels. These artists had been holding annual exhibits since 1884 and frequently invited nontraditional artists from other countries to join them. Monet, Morisot, Pissarro, and

Cézanne's landscapes, such as *Mont Sainte-Victoire with Large Pine-Tree* (1887), were ignored when they were exhibited in the 1890 exhibition in Brussels that also featured a young Vincent van Gogh.

Renoir had all exhibited with the group. At first, Cézanne was reluctant to submit any work, but then relented. He submitted two landscapes and one of his *Bathers* studies, hoping this time his work would be appreciated. Unfortunately for Cézanne, the work of a new young artist, Vincent van Gogh, was also shown in the exhibit. Van Gogh's original technique and fragmented brushstrokes caused such a scandal that the work of most of the other exhibitors, including that of Cézanne, was ignored.

Cézanne was once again disappointed. For a second time, he turned his back on the art world, vowing to focus his attention on his experiments in depicting space and solidity. His work continued to change as he aged.

# The Final Years

Cézanne did not let the lack of response to his paintings deter him. He spent the remaining years of his life working. He was so intent on achieving his vision that he withdrew from the world. His work and his name were almost forgotten. Many people thought he was dead. But he was very much alive, painting from dawn to dusk until the day he died. Even in his old age, his painting style continued to change. His work became simpler and more abstract, focusing more on color, geometric shape, and balance than on the subject matter.

## Ill Health and Isolation

Until 1889, Cézanne restlessly moved between Aix and Paris. After that, he rarely left Aix. Consumed with work and often frustrated with the results, he became increasingly irritable and avoided personal contact. Sometimes when he saw friends on the street in Paris, he lowered his eyes in an attempt to avoid them, or he made gestures pleading with them to pass him by. Both Guillaumin and Monet reported such occurrences.

Making matters worse, he developed diabetes in 1890. The disease lowered his energy and seemed to make him even crankier. Almost anything could set him off. For instance, in an effort to cheer him up, Monet organized a party in Cézanne's honor. Although Cézanne went to the party, he did not stay long. According to John Rewald, Monet welcomed Cézanne by saying: "At last we are all here together and are happy to seize the occasion to tell you how fond we are of you and how much we admire your art." Dismayed, Cézanne stared at his friend. "You, too, are making fun of me!" were his only words. He turned and took his coat and left.[56]

As the years went by, Cézanne lost touch with his old friends. Yet they remained devoted to him, respecting his moodiness and need for solitude.

## The Hermit of Aix

Cézanne was happiest and most at peace at Jas de Bouffan. There, he maintained his own wing of the estate. His aged mother, whom he lovingly cared for when she was too weak to look after herself, lived in a separate wing. He often worked in the gardens painting the rows of stately chestnut trees. He painted still lifes in his messy attic studio. He also paid day laborers who worked on the family estate to act as models. Between 1890 and 1895, he painted a series of five paintings known as *The Card Players* using workers as his models. The paintings, which all portray men playing cards, are among Cézanne's most acclaimed works. The canvases vary in size and in the number of subjects. As the series progressed, Cézanne made the paintings smaller and simpler, reducing the number of figures from five to two and playing down the background. Art critic Richard Dorment looks at this progression:

> All we can do is stand back and watch the artist's thought process over a span of five years, as he casts a critical eye over a finished canvas, decided that he can do something to improve it, starts another canvas, fails again, but fails better. Moving from picture to picture, we can see how he corrects and strengthens perceived

weaknesses, as in each attempt he tries to find monumentality, simplicity, and pictorial unity.[57]

In creating the paintings, Cézanne made over a dozen detailed sketches and watercolor studies of the individual models. From these he constructed the actual compositions, incorporating the figures into a carefully planned scene. For Cézanne, the series was more an experiment in depicting figures in space, and the relationship between color and form, than an attempt to portray actual people. The subjects could have been anyone. "To him, a head was no different than an apple as the basis for a composition; for Cézanne was not interested in emotions or individual personalities of any of the people whose portraits he painted,"[58] Becks-Malorny explains.

Cézanne's concern with balance and composition led him to reduce the number of figures from five to two in his painting series *The Card Players* (1890–1895).

One of Cézanne's main concerns was creating a balanced composition, which is why he reduced the number of subjects to two. He used color to unify the paintings. His method of distorting perspective also added balance and unity. Everything he did was carefully calculated. A line in one direction is offset by a line in another. For instance, one man is thin while the other is chunky; the table slants downward and the wall behind it slants upward. As he pared down each painting, Cézanne experimented with using geometric forms to shape his subjects and give the compositions volume and balance. As Cézanne explained to a young artist: "Everything in nature is modeled after the sphere, the cone, and the cylinder."[59]

All of this was quite innovative. According to Dorment, "What Cézanne is doing in the later canvases is unprecedented. When they were finally shown after Cézanne's death, they opened the gateway to cubism."[60]

## Young Artists Take Note

Resigned to obscurity, Cézanne remained isolated, and his later paintings, like *The Card Players*, were largely unseen. Despite his withdrawal from the art world, young artists who visited Tanguy's shop were beginning to develop an appreciation for his work. To some degree, Cézanne's isolation and his refusal to exhibit his work made him seem mysterious. A mystique grew up around him among a new generation of artists who were breaking away from Impressionism and exploring a more modern way to express themselves. They admired Cézanne's rebellious independence as well as his artistic innovations. As Maurice Denis, one of these young artists, wrote in 1907:

> The mystery in which the Master of Aix-en-Provence has surrounded his life, only helps to deepen the obscurity of commentaries, which, nonetheless, benefit his fame. He was timid, independent, and solitary. Exclusively occupied with his art, perpetually worried, and most often dissatisfied with himself, he escaped

public curiosity until his last years. The author of these pages admits that around 1890 at the time of his first visits to Tanguy's shop, he thought Cézanne was a myth, maybe even a pseudonym for an artist who specialized in other things, and he doubted his existence.[61]

Journalists, art critics, art collectors, and owners of small art galleries, which were beginning to pop up in the early 1890s, were beginning to take notice, too. Many began visiting Tanguy's shop just to view the Cézannes.

The *Lac d'Anney* dates from 1896. As Cézanne became more isolated, his work was becoming more popular.

# Cézanne Speaks

*Cézanne wrote letters to other artists throughout his life and towards the end of his life held conversations with young artists who came to him for advice. Much of what he said has been preserved. Here are some of his most famous pronouncements:*

"Art has a harmony which parallels that of nature."

"Color is the place where our brain and the universe meet."

"I don't think of anything when I paint. I see colors. I strive with joy to convey them on to my canvas just as I see them."

"Color is alive and color alone makes things come alive. . . . These colors in the scattered fields signify an idea to me, just as to them they signify a crop. Confronted by a yellow, they spontaneously feel the harvesting activity required of them, just as I, when faced with the same ripening tint."

"All tones interpenetrate; all forms . . . interlock. This is coherence."

"Art must make nature eternal in our imagination."

"We must not paint what we think we see, but what we see."

*Famous Artists and Great Painters.* www.quotes-famous-artists.org/paul-cezanne-famous-quotes.

In 1894, when Tanguy died, his art collection was auctioned off. Ambroise Vollard, a young art dealer and small gallery owner of avant-garde, or modern, unconventional art, attended the auction. When he saw Cézanne's work, he said: "I felt as though I had been punched in the stomach."[62] He snapped up six of the artist's paintings. Gustave Geffroy, an influential art critic, also attended the auction. He, too, was wowed by Cézanne's work, and wrote an article praising Cézanne, which appeared in a prestigious art journal.

# A One Man Show

Interest in Cézanne's work was on the rise. Pissarro, Renoir, and Monet urged Vollard to seize the moment and hold an exhibit of their friend's work. The prospect was risky. Cézanne's work had not been well received in the past, and Vollard was just starting his career. The success or failure of the show could make or destroy Vollard's reputation and his career. But Vollard was so taken by Cézanne's work that he was willing to take the risk. Before he could do so, the young art dealer had to get Cézanne's permission and more paintings to display. Vollard tracked Cézanne down through his son, Paul, in Paris, who wrote to his father urging him to exhibit.

In response, Cézanne sent Vollard 150 paintings, dating between 1868 and 1894. They were rolled up rather than stretched and nailed to a wood frame; some were torn and dirty; some appeared unfinished. Among them were a number of portraits, still lifes, landscapes, and paintings from the *Bathers* series, one of which Vollard displayed in the gallery's window. Because the gallery was small, Vollard exhibited fifty paintings at a time on a rotating basis.

# The Exhibition

The show attracted a huge amount of attention. As in the past, many exhibitiongoers came to gawk. But other visitors to the exhibit were quite enthusiastic. Among them were many young

Cézanne painted
*A Pyramid of Skulls*
at his studio in Aix
around 1900.

artists who were awed and inspired by Cézanne's work. The show, according to Rebecca Rabinow, curator of nineteenth-century painting at New York City's Metropolitan Museum of Art, "was a revelation to collectors, to artists, and instantly his work began to influence the next generation of artists. It had an immense impact."[63]

Even Cézanne's closest friends were overwhelmed. They had not seen Cézanne's more recent work. Renoir, Pissarro, Monet, Degas, and Julie Manet, Édouard Manet's widow, all bought paintings. In fact, Renoir and Degas drew lots to determine who would buy a particular still life that they both wanted. In the future, Cézanne would become known as a painter's painter, because his work was so appreciated by other artists.

A number of art collectors also snapped up paintings, while the press' response was varied. One reporter described the exhibit as a nightmare, while others were enchanted by Cézanne's work. Gustave Geffroy wrote:

> When the test has been made, and it is high time that it should be made, all that is obscure and legendary in Cézanne's career will be cleared up, and there will remain his work, severe but charming, and furthermore erudite [knowledgeable about art], powerful, yet simple. . . . His work will be hung in the Louvre and the collection contains more than one canvas which will enter museums of the future.[64]

## Cézanne and Vollard Meet

Cézanne did not attend the exhibit. He remained in Aix. In 1896, Vollard traveled there to meet Cézanne and to purchase more of his paintings. Cézanne's son went along to make sure the reclusive artist would receive the art dealer. Vollard and Cézanne got along well. Cézanne agreed to let Vollard be his art dealer. This arrangement made Vollard rich and Cézanne famous.

Vollard bought every painting Cézanne had in his studio. He also rescued a still life from a tree limb where Cézanne had flung it in frustration. The art dealer paid Cézanne 150 francs ($30) per painting. Vollard sold the paintings for double, triple, and even quadruple his purchasing price. Over the years, he would sell a total of 680 Cézannes.

Vollard also went around Aix buying Cézanne's paintings from the local people whom Cézanne had given them to, or who had picked them up in fields where Cézanne abandoned them. Cézanne's artwork was not appreciated in Aix. Yet the townspeople kept the paintings, usually in attics and storerooms, simply because they were free. Most jumped at the chance of selling them, laughing at the thought that people in Paris would actually pay for such atrocities.

# Growing Fame

Although the townspeople of Aix and conservative members of the traditional art establishment continued to deny Cézanne's talent, Vollard had little trouble selling the paintings he brought back from Aix. Artists and collectors of avant-garde art from all over the world were willing to pay increasingly higher prices for a Cézanne. In 1899, when Chocquet died, his art collection, which included work by all the original Impressionists, was sold. The average price per painting was 1,600 francs ($321), but Cézanne's *House of the Hanged Man, Auvers-sur-Oise* sold for 6,200 francs ($1,243), a large sum for the time. In addition, one of his landscapes sold for 6,750 francs ($1,354) to Monet.

Maurice Denis's 1900 painting *Homage to Cézanne* is one example of how much younger artists admired Cézanne.

The next year, despite the dismay of some traditionalists, three of Cézanne's paintings were prominently displayed at the 1900 Paris World's Fair. In 1901, twelve of his paintings were exhibited in Berlin. It was the first time the artist's work was seen in Germany. German poet Rainer Maria Rilke was so inspired by Cézanne's paintings that he later wrote a famous series of essays about Cézanne's artwork.

Rilke was not the only one inspired by Cézanne. In 1901, Cézanne exhibited at the Salon of Independent Artists in Paris. Young artist Maurice Denis also participated in the show. He exhibited a large painting entitled *Homage to Cézanne*. In the painting, a group of young artists, including Denis, Odilon Redon, and Édouard Vuillard, are respectfully gathered around an easel holding a still life by Cézanne. Denis's painting was the first public demonstration of how much Cézanne meant to these young artists. It was much talked about in the press. Cézanne wrote to Denis, thanking the young artist for honoring him. Denis wrote back: "Perhaps you will now have some idea of the place you occupy in the painting of our time, of the admiration you inspire, and of the enlightened enthusiasm of a few young people, myself included, because it is to you they are indebted to for whatever they have understood about painting; and we will never be able to thank you enough for it."[65]

In the next few years, Cézanne's work was exhibited in Belgium, England, Paris, Austria, Germany, and even in Aix, where he listed himself as "a student of Pissarro," in honor of his old friend and mentor. In 1904, thirty-three of his paintings were exhibited in the Salon of Independent Artists in Paris, where a whole room was dedicated to the artist. That same year, one of his landscapes sold to an American collector for an unprecedented 15,000 francs ($3,009).

# Cézanne's Mountain

The painting that the American collector bought was one in a series of seventy-five paintings of Mont Sainte-Victoire, a subject that occupied Cézanne for the last fifteen years of his life.

*Mont Sainte-Victoire* (1902) shows how Cézanne's later work became more abstract.

To Cézanne, the mountain, which was part of a mountain chain that cut through southern France, represented the essence of Aix.

In 1897, after Cézanne's mother died, Cézanne and his sisters sold Jas de Bouffan. Cézanne rented a room in an old estate in a pine forest near Mont Sainte-Victoire. From there, he had an excellent view of the mountain. A few years later, Cézanne bought a piece of land in the hills north of Aix and built a small house with a studio there. Here, he had a different view of the mountain.

The artist took full advantage of both vistas. He painted the mountain from every angle and distance, creating a new version of the landscape on each canvas. The mountain and the land around it, with its varied geometric shapes and colors, was a perfect subject for the artist. Upon seeing the series in 1907,

Rilke wrote: "Not since Moses, has anyone seen a mountain so greatly."[66]

As the years went by, Cézanne's depiction of the mountain and the surrounding landscape became more and more simplified until the series began to resemble modern abstract art. The mountain and its surroundings appear more like masses of color and shapes than realistic portrayals of the scenery. From his studies of nature, Cézanne came to believe that the eye sees patches of color, which the mind interprets and names. In his paintings of Mont Sainte-Victoire, Cézanne wanted to record only what his eyes saw, not what his mind identified. For this reason, from 1900 onward, objects in his paintings become less and less discernible, disintegrating into overlapping patches of color. It is hard to distinguish houses from trees, or where the mountain ends and the sky begins. Cézanne divided the compositions into three horizontal areas. In the foreground (at the bottom of the canvas), vertical brushstrokes in varying shades of green represent trees. In the middle, cubes form houses, and flat horizontal yellow and brown brushstrokes hint at fields of wheat. In the background (at the top of the canvas), a blue and green cone forms the mountain, and small brushstrokes in transparent layers of blue intermingle with patches of white canvas to form the sky. As art historian Frederico Zeri wrote: "Cézanne paints the elements of the landscape by inserting them into one chromatic [colorful] network; every individual image disappears in the vision of the whole, every shape becomes purely a link in the overall harmony of colors."[67]

# "I Have Sworn to Die Painting"

Although Cézanne was finally a successful artist, he did not change the way he lived. He remained a recluse in Aix, endlessly searching for the best way to express the essence of nature. At times he was satisfied with his work; at other times he felt he would never achieve his vision. As he wrote Vollard in 1903: "I work obstinately, and once in a while I catch a glimpse of the

Promised Land. Am I to be like the great leader of the Hebrews [Moses, who did not reach the biblical promised land], or will I really attain unto it? . . . I have made some progress. Oh, why so late and so painful?"[68]

He went out to paint no matter the weather or the state of his health. He also worked tirelessly in his studio on his *Bathers* series, spending many years on *The Large Bathers* (1900–1905), which is considered to be a masterpiece of modern art. In it, Cézanne uses repeated colors to merge the figures of the eleven bathers with each other and the landscape. He purposefully ignores human anatomy. The bathers' bodies are based on elongated or rounded geometric shapes. Cézanne has reduced them to simple forms without faces or individuality. The perspective, too, is distorted. The painting has a very modern feel, much

Cézanne's *The Large Bathers* (1900–1905)—one of several paintings of his from this period with the same subject matter and title—feels very modern.

# CÉZANNE AND CUBISM

Cézanne's paintings greatly influenced the Cubists. Cubism is a style of painting that developed in the early 1900s. Its leaders were Pablo Picasso (1881–1973) and Georges Braque (1882–1963).

The Cubists tried to create a new way of seeing things. They were concerned with the basic geometric shapes of things. They were unconcerned with traditional perspective. Instead, they wanted to show all sides of an object in the same picture. They did this by decomposing or fracturing three-dimensional objects. Some of their paintings look as if they were cut up and then crudely pasted back together.

The early Cubists used only a few colors in their paintings. As time went on, they added more color. Picasso also added paper and cloth to his canvases, turning them into collages.

In some Cubist paintings it is easy to distinguish the subject. Others are extremely abstract and appear more like lines, colors, and shapes.

like the Mont Sainte-Victoire series. It is opening the door to a new form of art defined by color and shape. In fact, the painting influenced Pablo Picasso's controversial 1907 painting *The Young Ladies of Avignon*, which also depicts distorted, elongated nude figures.

Cézanne would not live to see Picasso's painting. On October 15, 1906, he got caught in a storm while painting outdoors. Drenched to the bone and weakened by diabetes, he collapsed on the road while dragging his art supplies home. He was picked up by a laundry cart. Badly weakened, he developed

A Sotheby's staff member displays Cézanne's *Pichet et fruits sur une table* at an auction in 2010. The painting was sold for approximately $16.5 million.

pneumonia. Despite his condition, he refused to stay in bed and continued painting. "I have sworn to die painting,"[69] he wrote to a friend a few weeks earlier. On October 22, he died as he had sworn to die.

## Cézanne's Legacy

Interest in Cézanne's work skyrocketed after his death. In 1907, a show held in Paris featuring fifty-six of his paintings greatly influenced many young painters and the direction art would take in the twentieth century. Cézanne's use of color and simplified subject matter inspired artists like Paul Gauguin, Henri Matisse, and Charles Camoin. His exploration of geometric shapes and multiple perspectives led artists like Pablo Picasso, Georges Braque, and Juan Gris to experiment with more complex multiple views of the same subject and eventually to the fracturing of form, in which objects are depicted as overlapping geometric solids. According to an article on the Worldwide Art Gallery website:

The art of Paul Cézanne is considered today as being of enormous importance to the development of modern art. From his search for underlying structure of the composition came Cubism and then Abstraction. Cézanne's use of color as tone and his obsession with the formal elements of composition made it possible for artists who came after to question what they saw and how they represented what they saw on their canvas.[70]

A few weeks before his death, Cézanne wrote his son: "I continue to work with difficulty, but in spite of that something is achieved."[71] Cézanne did not live long enough to know how much he had achieved. This modest man, who often doubted his own ability, changed the future of art forever.

# Notes

## Introduction: A Visionary

1. Quoted in Gerstle Mack. *Paul Cézanne*. New York: Paragon House, 1989, p. 209.
2. Mack. *Paul Cézanne*, p. 108.
3. Quoted in John Rewald. *Cézanne*. New York: Harry N. Abrams, 1986, p. 186.
4. Mack. *Paul Cézanne*, p. 109.
5. Quoted in Paul Trachtman. "Cézanne: The man who changed the landscape of art." *Smithsonian*, January 2006, p. 80. www.smithsonianmag.com/arts-culture/cezanne06.html.
6. Quoted in Michael Doran, ed. *Conversations with Cézanne*. Berkeley: University of California Press, 2001, p. 181.
7. Quoted in www.paul-cezanne.org. "Paul Cezanne: The Complete Works." www.paul-cezanne.org.

## Chapter 1: An Emotional Young Man

8. Quoted in Mack. *Paul Cézanne*, p. 15.
9. Quoted in Trachtman. "Cézanne."
10. Quoted in Mack. *Paul Cézanne*, p. 31.
11. Quoted in Nicholas Wadley. *The Paintings of Cézanne*. New York: Mallard Press, 1989, pp. 9–10.

12. Quoted in Doran, ed. *Conversations with Cézanne*, p. 56.
13. Quoted in Rewald. *Cézanne*, p. 12.
14. Quoted in Rewald. *Cézanne*, pp. 25–26.
15. Quoted in Rewald. *Cézanne*, p. 29.
16. Quoted in Mack. *Paul Cézanne*, p. 107.
17. Quoted in Rewald. *Cézanne*, p. 33.
18. Rewald. *Cézanne*, p. 34.

## Chapter 2: Cézanne and the Impressionists

19. National Museums Liverpool. "'The Murder,' by Paul Cézanne." www.liverpoolmuseums.org.uk/picture-of-month/displaypicture.asp?venue=2&id=141.
20. Jim Lane. "The Salon des Refuses." Humanities Web.org. www.humanitiesweb.org/human.php?s=g&p=a&a=i&ID=293
21. Lane. "The Salon des Refuses."
22. Quoted in Rewald. *Cézanne*, p. 57.
23. Mack. *Paul Cézanne*, p. 124.
24. Quoted in Ulrike Becks-Malorny. *Paul Cézanne 1839–1906: Pioneer of Modernism*. Koln, Germany: Taschen, 2006, p. 16.
25. Becks-Malorny. *Paul Cézanne*, p. 20.
26. Quoted in Museum of Modern Art (MoMA). "Cézanne and Pissarro."

www.moma.org/explore/multimedia/audios/19/482.

27. Quoted in Becks-Malorny. *Paul Cézanne*, p. 21.

28. Jerry Saltz. "Unequal Partners." Artnet.com. www.artnet.com/magazine/reviews/saltz/saltz6-27-05.asp.

29. Leo J. O'Donovan. "Mutual Teachers: The Story of Two Rebels with a Common Purpose: To Reinvent the World of Art." *America*, August 29, 2005, p. 20.

## Chapter 3: "I Want to Make of Impressionism Something Solid and Durable"

30. Quoted in Doran, ed. *Conversations with Cézanne*, p. 22.

31. Quoted in Musée d'Orsay. "Paul Cézanne: *A Modern Olympia*." www.musee-orsay.fr/en/collections/works-in-focus/search/commentaire/commentaire_id/une-moderne-olympia-20438.html?no_cache=1&cHash=99368eeff3.

32. Quoted in Mack. *Paul Cézanne*, p. 191.

33. Quoted in Doran, ed. *Conversations with Cézanne*, p. xxvii.

34. Quoted in Wadley. *The Paintings of Cézanne*, p. 99.

35. Becks-Malorny. *Paul Cézanne*, p. 37.

36. Mack. *Paul Cézanne*, p. 209.

37. Quoted in Doran, ed. *Conversations with Cézanne*, p. 122.

38. Quoted in Trachtman. "Cézanne."

39. Peter Schjeldahl. "Game Change." *New Yorker*, February 28, 2011, p. 78.

40. Quoted in Doran, ed. *Conversations with Cézanne*, p. 110.

41. Quoted in Rewald. *Cézanne*, p. 146.

42. Quoted in Wadley. *The Paintings of Cézanne*, p. 37.

43. Quoted in Doran, ed. *Conversations with Cézanne*, p. 39.

## Chapter 4: "I Will Astonish Paris with an Apple"

44. Quoted in Francoise Cachin, Isabelle Cahn, Walter Feilchenfeldt, Henri Loyrette, Joseph J. Rishel. *Cézanne*. New York: Harry N. Abrams, 1996, p. 184.

45. Quoted in Cachin, Cahn, Feilchenfeldt, Loyrette, Rishel. *Cézanne*, p. 222.

46. Becks-Malorny. *Paul Cézanne*, p. 75.

47. Nancy Doyle Fine Art. "Artist Profile: Paul Cézanne." www.ndoylefineart.com/cezanne.html.

48. Nancy Doyle Fine Art. "Artist Profile: Paul Cézanne."

49. Quoted in Cachin, Cahn, Feilchenfeldt, Loyrette, Rishel. *Cézanne*, p. 29.

50. Quoted in Ambroise Vollard. *Cézanne*. New York: Dover, 1984, p. 74.

51. Quoted in Doran, ed. *Conversations with Cézanne*, pp. 9–10.

52. Quoted in Doran, ed. *Conversations with Cézanne*, p. 6.

53. Quoted in Cachin, Cahn, Feilchenfeldt, Loyrette, Rishel. *Cézanne*, p. 34.

54. Quoted in Wadley. *The Paintings of Cézanne*, p. 51.

55. Quoted in Radek Stencl. "Paul Cézanne, Still Life with Apples—Study." www.radekstencl.com/articles/study-paul-cezanne-still-life-with-apples.

## Chapter 5: The Final Years

56. Quoted in Rewald. *Cézanne*, p. 188.

57. Richard Dorment. "Paul Cézanne:

The Card Players, Courtauld Gallery, review." *Telegraph*, October 25, 2010. www.telegraph.co.uk/culture/art /art-reviews/8086198/Paul-Cézanne -The-Card-Players-Courtauld-Gal lery-review.html.

58. Becks-Malorny. *Paul Cézanne*, p. 62.
59. Quoted in Cachin, Cahn, Feilchenfeldt, Loyrette, Rishel. *Cézanne*, p. 18.
60. Dorment. "Paul Cézanne."
61. Quoted in Doran, ed. *Conversations with Cézanne*, p. 166.
62. Quoted in Musée d'Orsay. "From Cézanne to Picasso, Masterpieces from the Vollard Gallery." www .musee-orsay.fr/en/events/exhibi tions/in-the-musee-dorsay/exhibi tions-in-the-musee-dorsay/article /chefs-doeuvre-de-la-galerie-vol lard-4258.html?cHash=bab1b8a624.
63. Quoted in Susan Stamberg. "The Art of the Dealer: 'From Cézanne to Picasso.'" NPR.com, October 17, 2006. www.npr.org/templates/story /story.php?storyId=6279921.
64. Quoted in Mack. *Paul Cézanne*, p. 342.
65. Quoted in Cachin, Cahn, Feilchenfeldt, Loyrette, Rishel. *Cézanne*, p. 34.
66. Quoted in Trachtman. "Cézanne."
67. Paul Cézanne, Federico Zeri, Marco Dolchetta. *Cézanne Mont Sainte-Victoire*. Ontario, Canada: NDE Publishing, 2000, p. 11.
68. Quoted in Vollard. *Cézanne*, p. 103.
69. Quoted in Rewald. *Cézanne*, p. 263.
70. The Worldwide Art Gallery. "Paul Cezanne (1839–1906)." www.theart gallery.com.au/cezanne.html.
71. Quoted in Rewald. *Cézanne*, p. 263.

# Glossary

**abstract art:** An artistic style in which objects are depicted differently than they actually appear in the natural world. Therefore, the subject may be largely unrecognizable.

balance: When the scale, proportions, shapes, and colors in an artwork are evenly organized and placed.

Cubism: An artistic style in which objects are represented by geometric forms, which are simultaneously depicted from multiple angles.

Impressionism: An artistic style depicting a moment in time that uses bright colors to depict light.

landscape: A work of art that depicts the outdoors.

linear **perspective:** A method of showing depth in art by directing parallel lines towards the horizon and depicting close objects as larger than far objects.

**modelling:** A way to show depth in art by using light to dark shading.

motif: The theme or central pattern in a piece of art or literature.

multiple **perspective:** A method of showing depth in a painting by showing an object from more than one angle.

Neoclassicism: An artistic style based on classical Greek and Roman art and stories.

palett**e knife:** A spatula-like tool used to apply or remove paint.

perspective: The technique artists use to depict depth.

primary **colors:** The three colors that other colors are derived from: red, yellow, and blue.

**Realism:** An artistic style using common people and everyday scenes as subjects.

**Romanticism:** An artistic style emphasizing emotions painted in a dramatic manner.

still **life:** A work of art that depicts inanimate objects such as fruit.

# For More Information

## Books

Robert Burleigh. *Paul Cézanne: A Painter's Journey*. New York: Harry N. Abrams, 2006. This book gives an overview of Cézanne's life, photos of the artist, examples of his paintings from all stages of his life with discussions of the work, and examples of paintings of Cézanne's contemporaries.

Nathaniel Harris. *Cézanne*. New York: Franklin Watts, 2006. This title looks at Cézanne's life and struggles. It includes a historical time line, photos, examples of Cézanne's paintings, and information about where Cézanne's work can be seen.

Peggy J. Parks. *Impressionism*. Farmington Hills, MI: Lucent Books, 2006. This illustrated book provides a close look at the Impressionist movement, what it is, how it developed, the reaction to it, and its effects on art.

Kathleen Tracy. *Paul Cézanne*. Hockessin, Delaware: Mitchell Lane, 2007. This book looks at Cézanne's life, his friendship with Émile Zola, Impressionism, and Cézanne's artwork. It contains examples of his paintings, a chronology of his life, and a historical time line.

Mike Venezia. *Paul Cézanne*. New York: Children's Press, 1998. This simple book looks at Cézanne's life, some of his paintings, and the paintings of other artists who influenced him. It includes humorous cartoons and a list of where Cézanne's work can be seen today.

## Websites

**The Art Story.org: Paul Cézanne** (www.theartstory.org/artist-cezanne-paul.htm). This website looks at Cezanne's life, work, and legacy, with statements by the artist, key ideas about his painting style, and an interactive chart on the people and art forms that influenced him and those he influenced.

**Atelier Cézanne** (www.atelier-cezanne .com/anglais/visites.htm). This website takes viewers on a virtual tour of Cézanne's last studio. It provides a time line of the artist's life, reproductions of his work, information on Mont Sainte-Victoire, and a virtual tour of places in Aix that figured prominently in Cézanne's life.

**National Gallery of Art: Cézanne in Provence.** (www.nga.gov/exhibitions/2006/cezanne/index.shtm). A web resource from the National Gallery of Art includes archival material from past Cézanne exhibits, a guide to Cézanne's works in their collection, and links to outside resources on the artist.

**Paul Cezanne: The Complete Works** (www.paul-cezanne.org). This website provides a brief biography, pictures of the artist's complete works, and numerous links.

**WebMuseum, Paris** (www.ibiblio.org/wm/paint/auth/cezanne). This website provides information on Cézanne's life, selected paintings, and how his painting style changed over time.

# Index

Salon and, 48–50
style, 68
Ingres, Jean-Auguste-Dominique, 24, 25
"The Inseparables," 16–17, 19, 57

**K**
Kandinsky, Wassily, 78

**L**
Lane, Jim, 33–34
*L'artiste* (journal), 50
Linear perspective, 66–69
Louvre, 27, 33, 44, 57, 61, 91

**M**
Mack, Gerstle, 9, 10–11, 37, 59
Manet, Édouard,
Salon and, 36, 49–51
Salon des Refusés and, 37–38
*Luncheon on the Grass* (1863), 36–37, 37, 51
funeral, 65
*Olympia* (1865), 50, 51
use of color, 37
Manet, Julie, 90–91
Matisse, Henri, 12, 98
Metropolitan Museum of Art, 90
Modelling, 66–68
Monet, Claude
art exhibitions and, 81
Batignolles Group and, 37–38
Cézanne, Paul and, 61, 72, 83–84, 89–91
*Impression, Sunrise* (1874), 51
Impressionist terminology and, 51–52
Manet, Édouard funeral and, 65
Society of Painters, Sculptors, and Engravers and, 49
Montifaud, Marc de, 50
Morisot, Berthe, 50, 57, 81, 82

**N**
Napoleon III, emperor of France, 36
Natanson, Thadée, 78–79

Neoclassic style, 17, 19, 24, 25, 30, 36
Nude portraits, 36–37, *37*

**O**
O'Donovan, Leo J., 45
Outdoor painting (*en plein air*), 12, 38, 44–45, 49

**P**
Picasso, Pablo, 6, 7, 12, 97, 98
Pissarro, Camille
art exhibitions and, 36, 81–82, 89
Batignolles Group and, 38
Cézanne, Paul and, 44–46, 48, 54, 57, 67, 72, 89, 90
*The Conversation, chemin du chou, Pontoise* (1874), 46–47
Corot, Camille and, 44
Pointillist painting style, 44
Postimpressionism, 68
Poussin, Nicolas, 25

**R**
Rabinow, Rebecca, 90
Raphael, 25, 51
Realistic art movement, 17, 31
Renaissance, 66
Renoir, Pierre-August
art exhibitions, 57, 81
Batignolles Group and, 37–39
Cézanne, Paul and, 52, 61, 72, 89–91
Impressionist style and, 51
Society of Painters, Sculptors, and Engravers and, 49
Rewald, John, 29, 84
Rivière, Georges, 56
Romantic art movement, 17, 19, 31

**S**
Salon, 32–36, 40, 48–50, 62–63
Salon des Refusés, 36–38, 48
Saltz, Jerry, 45
Schjeldahl, Peter, 61
Seurat, Georges, 44
Sisley, Alfred, 37, 49, 57

# Picture Credits

Cover: © Dennis Hallinan/Alamy
© Cameraphoto Arte, Venice/Art Resource, NY, 41
Courtesy National Gallery of Art, Washington, 22, 35, 53, 63, 70
Digital Image © The Museum of Modern Art/Licensed by SCALA/Art
    Resource, NY, 18
© Erich Lessing/Art Resource, NY, 9, 14, 21, 31, 37, 39, 43, 55, 74, 81, 87, 90
Image copyright © The Metropolitan Museum of Art/Art Resource, NY, 15
© Gianni Dagli Orti/The Art Archive at Art Resource, NY, 92
*The House at Jas de Bouffan*, 1882–1885 (oil on canvas), Cézanne, Paul (1839–
    1906)/Private Collection/Photo © Christie's Images/The Bridgeman Art
    Library, 11
*The House of the Hanged Man, Auvers-sur-Oise*, 1873 (oil on canvas), Cézanne,
    Paul (1839–1906)/Musee d'Orsay, Paris, France/Giraudon/The Bridgeman
    Art Library, 46
*Kitchen Table (Still life with basket)*, 1888–1890 (oil on canvas), Cézanne, Paul
    (1839–1906)/Musee d'Orsay, Paris, France/Giraudon/The Bridgeman Art
    Library, 79
*The Large Bathers*, c. 1900–1905 (oil on canvas), Cézanne, Paul (1839–1906)/
    National Gallery, London, UK/The Bridgeman Art Library, 96
*L'Estaque, View of the Bay of Marseilles*, c. 1878–1879 (oil on canvas), Cézanne,
    Paul (1839–1906)/Musee d'Orsay, Paris, France/Giraudon/The Bridgeman
    Art Library, 60
*A Modern Olympia*, 1873–1874 (oil on canvas), Cézanne, Paul (1839–1906)/
    Musee d'Orsay, Paris, France/Giraudon/The Bridgeman Art Library, 49
*Mont Sainte-Victoire*, c. 1902 (oil on canvas), Cézanne, Paul (1839–1906)/
    Philadelphia Museum of Art, Pennsylvania, PA, USA/The George W. Elkins
    Collection/The Bridgeman Art Library, 94

# About the Author

Barbara Sheen is the author of more than seventy-five books for young people. She lives in New Mexico with her family. In her spare time, she likes to swim, walk, garden, cook, and read. Writing about Cézanne has inspired her to take up painting.

Art
Bio
Cezanne